The Feminist Thought
of Sarah Grimké

THE FEMINIST

THOUGHT OF

Sarah Grimké

GERDA LERNER

New York   Oxford

OXFORD UNIVERSITY PRESS

1998

Oxford University Press

Oxford   New York
Athens   Auckland   Bangkok   Bogotá   Bombay
Buenos Aires   Calcutta   Cape Town   Dar es Salaam
Delhi   Florence   Hong Kong   Istanbul   Karachi
Kuala Lumpur   Madras   Madrid   Melbourne
Mexico City   Nairobi   Paris   Singapore
Taipei   Tokyo   Toronto   Warsaw
and associated companies in
Berlin   Ibadan

Copyright © 1998 by Gerda Lerner

Published by Oxford University Press
198 Madison Avenue, New York, New York 10016

Oxford is a registered trademark of Oxford University Press

Library of Congress Cataloging-in-Publication Data
Lerner, Gerda, 1920–
The feminist thought of Sarah Grimké / Gerda Lerner.
p. cm. Includes index.
ISBN 0-19-510604-0 (cloth). – ISBN 0-19-510605-9 (pbk.)
1. Grimké, Sarah Moore, 1792–1873.
2. Grimké, Sarah Moore, 1792–1873—Archives.
3. Feminism–United States—History—19th century.
4. Feminism—United States—History—19th century—Sources.
5. Women abolitionists—United States—History—19th century.
I. Grimké, Sarah Moore, 1792–1873. II. Title.
HQ1418.L47 1998   305.42'0973–dc21   97-42197

1 3 5 7 9 8 6 4 2

Printed in the United States of America
on acid-free paper

To the memory of

EVE MERRIAM

and

KAY CLARENBACH

Feminist pioneers, my sisters in struggle,
dear friends

CONTENTS

ARTICLES
by Gerda Lerner

ACKNOWLEDGMENTS

I am deeply indebted to the following institutions and their staffs for giving me access to their collections and permission to reprint selections from unpublished letters and documents pertaining to Sarah Grimké:

John Dann, Director, and Robin Cox, Curator of Manuscripts, The William L. Clements Library, University of Michigan, Ann Arbor. Their cooperation, scholarly insights and support of my work were most helpful to me.

Robert C. Ritchie, Director of Research, and Martin Ridge, Senior Research Associate, The Huntington Library, San Marino, Calif. Their support for and interest in my work and the fellowship support given by the Huntington Library made my research time productive and most enjoyable. The availability of many of the books read by Sarah Grimké was of great value to me in interpreting her thought.

Department of Rare Books and Manuscripts, Boston Public Library, for permission to reprint the Grimké Sisters' "Letter to Queen Victoria."

The State Historical Society of Wisconsin, Madison, for use of its superb collection of nineteenth-century newspapers.

I am grateful to Professor Carl Degler for his challenge of my ascription of the essay "Marriage," for his willingness to let me quote from his correspondence, and for many years of intellectually stimulating exchanges and discussions. Our longstanding friendship has been unimpaired by our occasional disagreements.

My profound thanks go to Sheldon Meyer, who has for several decades edited my books, and who undertook this last editorial task shortly before his retirement. I have been enriched and strengthened by our long collaboration and by his unfailing support for my work.

Joellyn Ausanka has copy-edited this book with meticulous care, great skill and patient attention. I am truly grateful for her contribution to this work.

NOTE ON EDITING

All the documents, except where otherwise noted, are from the Weld Manuscript, William L. Clements Library, Ann Arbor, Michigan, and are reprinted by permission of the Library.

Except where otherwise noted, the order of the original manuscript has been preserved. Minor changes in punctuation have been made to provide clarity. Ampersands have been replaced by "and." Sentence structure, including ungrammatical constructions and misspellings, has been retained in order to preserve the flavor of the original document. I have attempted to identify the quotations used by Grimké in the essays. When I have been able to identify them I have footnoted them; the others remain unidentified.

The Feminist Thought
of Sarah Grimké

INTRODUCTION

In the early 1960s, when I completed my dissertation on *the Grimké Sisters*, women's history was of interest to fewer than a dozen historians in the United States Biographies of women were few and far between and were usually written by non-academic writers. My dissertation manuscript was rejected by twenty-four commercial publishers, with several publishers heaping considerable praise on the book's quality, while regretting they could not publish it due to the common wisdom that books on women did not sell. When Houghton-Mifflin, the twenty-fifth publisher to whom I submitted the manuscript, accepted it, the editor requested only a few minor changes in the text but insisted that I change the title. My original title had been: *The Grimké Sisters from South Carolina: Rebels against Slavery and for Women's Rights*. The 1969 hardcover title omitted the last four words, and it was not until a paperback edition appeared in 1971, published by Schocken Books, that the original title was restored at my insistence.

The contempt in which work on women in history was held in the 1960s not only represented career obstacles for the few of us who ventured into that field, but also limited our training and our command of methodology. We had to rely mostly on primary sources, which is all to the good, but in interpreting them, we lacked the concepts and above all the context on which sound interpretation is based. We approached the history of women with the tools developed for doing the history of men. Today we know that although this is an adequate basis from which to start, it is not sufficient.

3

Over thirty years later, I have decided to revisit part of my earlier work to see what I might do with it on the basis of what I have learned in the intervening years. In writing a biography on two subjects, Sarah and Angelina Grimké, there was always the difficulty of balancing between them and distinguishing the unique contributions of one from those of the other. That difficulty was, in my case, exacerbated by the fact that all previous historians and biographers, as well as the sisters' contemporaries, had focused their attention on Angelina. She was the celebrated public speaker; she was the heroine of the antislavery movement. Possibly because her major written work had focused on antislavery, not on women's rights as such, her work had more often been analyzed and referred to in the work of historians. Sarah, on the other hand, was a poor public speaker, and her major writings were focused on women; she was considered to have no historical significance apart from her sister. I knew enough at the time of my writing of the biography to want to rectify this neglect of Sarah Grimké, but my difficulty was in interpreting her writing. Sarah's argument for the emancipation of women was almost entirely theological; her language was biblical; her images were derived from Christian iconography. I was not trained in theology and had only cursory knowledge of Christian thought; thus I found it difficult to comprehend her arguments. I could not "get into" her character for the longest time. In working on the biography, I finally decided I must steep myself in the intellectual context out of which she was writing, and, for several months, I read only material she might have read. I focused in particular on the antislavery journals and papers and on the Quaker publication *The Friend*. That proved helpful, and I was able to get a sense of Sarah's personal and intellectual development, which I tried to incorporate in the biography. Her psychological development and her growth as a thinker stand up well in my current reading of the biography, and I have no desire to change my interpretation.

In the thirty years since my work on the biography, I have used the Grimké material frequently in teaching and lecturing and have written several scholarly articles on the subject (see Articles 18 and 19). Over the years, the work of Sarah Grimké seemed to me to take on greater significance, and I felt increasing dissatisfaction with the treatment I had given her work in my biography. I was able to rectify this somewhat by publishing two of her formerly unpublished manuscripts with my comments.[1] But it was only after I completed my research and writing on seven hundred years of feminist Bible criticism that I began to see the true dimensions of Sarah Grimké's achievements.[2] Now when I can look back over the rise of feminist consciousness, the development of ideas by women about their own situation, I see Sarah Grimké not only as the first woman to write a coherent feminist argument in the United States, but also as a major feminist thinker.

It is interesting to note that since the publication of my biography there has been considerable scholarly work done on the Grimké sisters but only one book which focuses on Sarah Grimké. Ann Bartlett, in her excellent essays and headnotes to a collection of Sarah Grimké's work, seems to share my conviction that Sarah Grimké's contribution to the history of feminist theory needs upgrading. Bartlett did so by placing Grimké's thought "in the contexts of her life and times."[3] What I am attempting to do in this essay is to place Sarah Grimké's feminist thought in the context of the long history of women's feminist thought in Western civilization and to make it accessible to teachers, students and the general reader.

Sarah Moore Grimké (1792–1873) and her younger sister Angelina Grimké Weld (1805–1879) were the only white Southern women ever to become leading abolitionists. For a short period they both served as agents of the American Anti-Slavery Society. Angelina's reputation as a public speaker far exceeded that of her sister. During the period of their public activity (1837–1839) each wrote a path-breaking book and a number of important pamphlets. Angelina wrote *Letters to Catherine E. Beecher,* a strong antislavery argument emphasizing the role of women; Sarah wrote *Letters on the Equality of the Sexes and the Condition of Woman,* which is the first book written by an American presenting a fully developed woman's rights argument, ten years before the first woman's rights convention in Seneca Falls, N.Y.[4] Both sisters have been celebrated in history as pioneers of woman's rights and abolition. During their period of public activism and for some time thereafter the intellectual work of the sisters was so closely linked and connected that it is somewhat difficult to isolate their separate authorship and contributions. I will argue here that in light of their work over their full lifespan, it becomes evident that it was Sarah who developed an original and radical argument for woman's rights, whereas Angelina's emphasis was more on antislavery and on women's right to participate publicly in the campaign for abolition. During their lifetime Angelina's reputation and notoriety far exceeded that of her sister. I believe that we can fully measure Sarah Grimké's significance only if we look at her *entire* work and all her writings. It is for this reason that the selections in this book are more heavily weighted toward her later work.

Sarah Grimké, born in Charleston, S.C., was the sixth child and the second daughter of John and Mary Grimké. Her father, a Lieutenant-Colonel in the Revolutionary Army, served in the newly-formed state government of South Carolina and eventually rose in the state's judiciary to a position equivalent to that of Chief Justice. He was a man of wealth and social standing, a powerful planter and slaveholder. Her mother, Mary Smith, who gave birth to fourteen children, came from a wealthy, aristocratic family which boasted two colonial governors among its ancestry. Sarah was raised in luxury, her comfort assured by the services of slaves, including her own personal attendant. She had been horrified by the cruelty to slaves she witnessed as a child and attempted to teach her own young slave to read and write. When she was discovered and punished for breaking the laws of South Carolina, her discontent with living under the slave system became explicit. But there was, in her society, no outlet possible for such feelings. When her slave companion died after an illness some years later, Sarah was disconsolate and refused to have another personal servant.

She was educated by tutors together with her older brother Thomas, but was not allowed to learn Latin on the grounds that girls had no use for such knowledge. The year she was twelve, she experienced a deep crisis when Thomas left to study at Yale, while her pleas for further education were denied. Later in life, she expressed her bitterness over this incident in a letter:

> With me learning was a passion. . . . Had I received the education I craved and been bred to the profession of law, I might have been a useful member of society, and instead of myself and my property being taken care of, I might have been a protector of the helpless.[5]

Sarah's incipient rebellion was deflected by the birth of her youngest sister, Angelina. She became the child's godmother and took over her care, which for a time provided an outlet for her unused energy and talents. Angelina for decades called Sarah "Mother"; their lifelong relationship always bore the imprint of Sarah's early maternal role. As a young Southern woman Sarah was expected to enter society and contract a suitable marriage. She resisted this by experiencing a religious conversion which led to her renouncing all entertainments, balls and dancing parties. But she "backslid" several times. A personal encounter with a famed Presbyterian revival minister, the Rev. Henry Kollock, became for her "a providential sign." In a week of private conversations with him she experienced profound guilt and conversion to evangelical religion. Once again, she gave up all fripperies and entertainment and devoted herself to prayer, charitable visits to alms-houses and to good deeds. Still, again, she backslid. Remorse over her repeated sinfulness was raised to excessive proportions when her father fell seriously ill in 1818. Sarah regarded the illness as "the merciful interposition of providence" designed expressly to save her. Her sinfulness had caused her father's illness; her repentance would save him.

Sarah's religious struggles and "conversion" followed a pattern quite conventional for young upper-class women of her time. But Sarah took the experience further than did others; it became a turning point in her life. When the local doctors advised her father to consult a famed physician in Philadelphia, he chose Sarah to accompany him on this visit. She did so, carrying out a duty which ordinarily should have fallen to a wife or eldest son. The Philadelphia physician was a Quaker, and the Grimkés lodged in Quaker boardinghouses. The doctor despaired of a cure, and at his recommendation they went to the New Jersey seashore, where, two months later, John Faucheraud Grimké died, attended only by his daughter.

For Sarah the experience of nursing the dying man was formative. "We lived in the constant sacrifice of selfishness . . . and became friends indeed," she wrote in the diary she began during this period. "I may say that our attachment became strengthened day by day. I regard this as the greatest blessing next to my conversion that I have ever received from God."[6] It is worth noting how she links her conversion and the intimacy of her love and friendship with her father. Her conversion had resulted in her experiencing enormous guilt, even in blaming herself for her father's illness. By nursing him in his final illness, she felt relieved of that guilt. "Constant sacrifice of selfishness" was the vehicle for finding redemption and inner peace. It was an insight which would, for better or worse, dominate the next stage of her life.

Sarah stayed for several months in Philadelphia before returning by ship to Charleston. On board, she met Israel Morris, a Philadelphia commission merchant, father of eight children and member of a highly respected and prosperous Quaker family. He introduced her to the principles of Quaker belief and gave her a copy of the writings of John Woolman, the Quaker minister who had preached against the sin of slavery in the South.

Back home Sarah felt like a stranger, more strongly than ever repelled by the daily experiences of the slave system. The simplicity of life she had observed among the Quakers made the luxury of her own surroundings seem intolerable. Yet she could see no way out and, typically, she experienced her turmoil in religious terms. Later, she described her state of mind:

> I cannot without shuddering look back to that period . . . Nothing interested me; I fulfilled my duties without any feeling of satisfaction, in gloomy silence. My lips moved in prayer, my feet carried me to the holy sanctuary, but my heart was estranged from piety. I felt as if my doom was irrevocably fixed, and I was destined to that fire which is never quenched. I have never experienced any feeling so terrific as the despair of salvation. My soul still remembers the wormwood and the gall, still remembers how awful the conviction that every door of hope was closed, and that I was given over to death.[7]

What she describes here is "the dark night of the soul," which many mystics describe just prior to their mystical experiences. In Sarah's case, it was the reading of John Woolman's autobiography which pointed her way. His strong antislavery convictions and actions became her challenge and example. Perhaps Quakerism would be the answer for her. After many months of correspondence with Israel Morris, in which he encouraged her to become a Quaker, she began to worship at a Quaker meeting-house in Charleston. The ridicule and disapproval of her family and friends for taking even this small step were an indication of what her life at home would be like should she persist in this course.

It was then that Sarah had mystical experiences. She heard voices, "she saw and communed with spirits, and did not hesitate to acknowledge their influence and to respect their intimations." She felt called to the Quaker ministry but recoiled and tried "to hide herself from the Lord." In one Quaker meeting she felt called upon to speak, but she trembled in fear and kept silent. Remorse overwhelmed her, and she felt she had sinned against God's command. This act of disobedience was one she would have on her conscience for many years. Meanwhile, she recorded and interpreted her dreams and visions, and with Israel Morris's frequent admonition to listen to her inner voice, she finally perceived an unmistakable command. Through her visions, she found the courage to defy her family, break with her upbringing, leave the comfort of home and wealth. Sarah Grimké would leave the land of slavery and go North to become a Quaker minister.[8]

In my biography, I treated these events as I then understood them: as a sort of unconscious strategy on Sarah's part in order to win her mother's approval for her highly unusual decision. Since then I have studied the experiences and life courses of female mystics over a period of seven hundred years. It is striking to note how similar are the circumstances under which many of them first have these mystical experiences. The death of a loved person, a near-death experience of their own, severe trauma in childbirth, or an incident of extreme violence often produce these manifestations. The mystic prior to having the visions, is deeply troubled, unhappy, sleepless, desperate. Then come the visions and with them a sense of release and inner peace.

Sarah had experienced such a period of inner turmoil, even depression. Like so many women before her, out of the depth of a sense of helplessness and despair she was lifted by mystic experiences to a state in which, for once, she could act. Unknowingly following the path of Hildegard of Bingen and the woman who was later to become Sarah's heroine, Joan of Arc, Sarah Grimké followed a well-trodden path to self-empowerment when she convinced her contemporaries that her voices were real.

Her departure was eased by her mother's acquiescence and by the pretense that it was a temporary trip undertaken for her health. In May 1821, Sarah, accompanied by her widowed sister Anna Frost and Anna's young daughter, sailed for Philadelphia. There she temporarily accepted Israel Morris's hospitality and then moved in with his sister, Catherine Morris. Two years later, in 1823, she was formally accepted as a member of the Arch Street Meeting of the Society of Friends. Although she would return for several brief visits to her hometown, Sarah's break with the South was final.

Supported by a modest income from her inheritance, Sarah lived in a restricted social circle from 1823 to 1829, dependent for friendship and contacts on the Orthodox Quaker elite of which the Morris family was an important part. This meant that Sarah was under the influence and tutelage of the most conservative group of Quakers, during a time when the Society of Friends was rent by dissension and factional struggles, which in 1828 resulted in the splitting off of the Hicksite group. There is no telling how her life would have developed, if she had been free to mingle with the liberal Hicksite Quakers, at least one of whom, Lucretia Mott, was closer to her in antislavery sympathies and incipient feminist thought than any of the group of people with whom she then lived.

During these years Sarah struggled first to accept the calling to the Quaker ministry and then to gain recognition for that calling on the part of the Quaker Monthly Meeting. Recognition that "a gift to the ministry had been committed to this person" was usually based on the response of the members, especially the Elders, to the candidate's extemporaneous utterances during worship. Sarah had, from the start, encountered hostility and suspicion on the part of some of the most influential Orthodox Quaker leaders, which found expression in their disparaging remarks whenever she rose to speak in Meeting. By nature shy and by long training accustomed to self-disparagement, Sarah was devastated by this response. She struggled with doubts and feelings of unworthiness for many years, to the point where attendance at Meetings became a torture for her.

Her struggle for acceptance by the Orthodox leaders was also mixed up with her struggle to break her dependency on Israel Morris, who had become not only her mentor and spiritual guide but the man she loved. Israel Morris had become a widower in 1820; with the youngest of his children then only five years old, it was only natural that, once Sarah had become a Quaker, he would consider her a suitable candidate for marriage. He proposed marriage to her in 1826 and was rejected. "That was a day of solemn, heart-felt supplication that nothing might intervene between me and my God . . . to the individual there was sufficient attachment, but my soul shrunk from the fearful responsibility of the situation," Sarah confided to her diary.⁹ Four years after he made his first proposal of marriage, Israel Morris repeated it and was again rejected. It is unclear from the record whether Sarah's rejection of him was based on her idea that she could not combine the role of minister with that of wife, or whether it was due to her fear of the pronounced opposition of his children and siblings to the marriage. At any rate, she refused him and struggled for many years to free herself from her love of him and to deny her feelings. There are hints in the record that indicate that Israel Morris was also conflicted about the relationship and gave her mixed signals. At any event, Sarah was unable for over nine years to disentangle her emotions for him from her sense of religious calling. Knowing the direction in which she would finally turn, it is highly suggestive that her rejection of marriage was also motivated by a desire for independence which she dared not acknowledge even to herself.¹⁰

During the years of Sarah's lonely struggle for a vocation, her sister Angelina found her own way out of the South. Her childhood, under Sarah's protection, had been sheltered and happy and had enabled Angelina to develop her outgoing, strong personality. Possibly under Sarah's influence Angelina early came to abhor slavery, but unlike her sister she acted on her convictions and asserted them confidently. Angelina's conversion from Episcopalianism to Presbyterianism was accomplished easily, and she threw herself into church work with great enthusiasm. She soon caused considerable conflict in the church by insisting that her minister preach against slavery. When he refused, she appeared at a meeting of the Elders of her church and suggested that they, as a body, should speak out against slavery. They refused, of course. Disillusioned, and impressed by Sarah's teaching of Quaker doctrine when she visited Charleston in 1827, Angelina decided to become a Quaker. But the tiny congregation in Charleston offered her neither support nor spiritual guidance, and Angelina continued to make a nuisance of herself with her family and friends on the subject of slavery. In November 1829, with her mother's consent, Angelina Grimké went North to join her sister and to become an exile.

From that time on and for the rest of their lives, except for one brief period of separation, the sisters lived together. They shared living space and recreation, read the same books, discussed each other's writings, shared correspondence with friends and frequently copied each other's manuscripts.[11] Angelina joined the same Quaker Meeting as Sarah and elicited the same hostility in her aspirations for the ministry as had her sister. But Angelina met these difficulties with her usual cheerful practicality; rather than becoming discouraged over her own failings, she found fault with the Quakers. It was she who first of the two sisters turned to organized antislavery in her search for a field of usefulness.

She became publicly associated with the abolitionist cause in 1835, when a private letter she had written to William Lloyd Garrison supporting his views was published in *The Liberator*.[12] Pressured by Philadelphia Quakers to renounce her letter, Angelina refused.

Meanwhile, after ten years of misery, Sarah had finally conquered her passion for Israel Morris and regained the self-confidence necessary to free herself from Quaker orthodoxy. When in 1836, on yet another occasion when she rose to pray aloud in Quaker Meeting, the Elder Jonathan Edwards interrupted her prayer and bade her sit down, she reacted quite differently than she had previously.

> I never felt more peaceful, and the conviction then arose that my bonds were broken. The act on the part of this Elder was entirely unprecedented and unsanctioned by our Discipline but his power is undisputed. I cannot give thee any idea of the spiritual bondage I have been in . . . but that has past [passed].[13]

She felt herself released from the ministry. The sisters each went through her own crisis, independent of the other, but both concluded that they had to leave the household of Catherine Morris, possibly even to leave Philadelphia. But where to live was a problem, since they had no friends outside the Orthodox Quaker circle. For the summer of 1836 each accepted invitations to stay with friends in New Jersey, once again separate from the other.

While she stayed at Mary Parker's house in Shrewsbury, N.J., Angelina found an inspired solution to her problems. She would write a pamphlet addressed to Southern women. She began at once and within two weeks had written her powerful *Appeal to the Christian Women of the South*, a unique attempt to draw Southern white women into the antislavery cause.[14] She conceived this work entirely on her own; Sarah did not even read the manuscript before Angelina sent it off to Elizur Wright at the American Anti-Slavery Society (hereafter AASS). The response was instant and enthusiastic. Not only would the Society print the pamphlet at once, but Wright invited her to come to New York and hold parlor meetings with women to bring them into the antislavery cause. Knowing that such a move would be opposed by Orthodox Quakers and might mean expulsion from the Society of Friends, Angelina hesitated.

Sarah joined her at Shrewsbury, and the sisters had a long and painful discussion. Sarah tried her best to dissuade Angelina from working in public for the Anti-slavery Society. She feared the inevitable outrage, censure, gossip, and even the possibility of violence. But Angelina had already decided to accept Wright's invitation to lecture in New York; she would go with Sarah or, if Sarah did not wish to join her, with her friend Jane Smith. After much inner struggle, Sarah's love for her sister outweighed her scruples, and she decided to go with her, even though she felt no calling for any kind of public role. Typically, she thought of herself only as Angelina's "auxiliary." Both sisters defied the opposition of Philadelphia Quakers, moved to New York City and shortly thereafter became the first two female agents of the American Anti-slavery Society.

This event became the second turning point in Sarah Grimké's life. She had helped her sister to a more positive and carefree childhood than she herself had had. She had converted Angelina to Quakerism, setting her on the path to antislavery. Now it was Angelina who helped her find a practical outlet for her long-held antislavery convictions. In a sense, it was Angelina who turned her away from mysticism and a purely religious quest to the work of the radical agent of social change.

Once in New York, the sisters were invited to join the Agents' Convention of the AASS, which was held in November 1836. An unprecedented organizational effort to systematically train forty antislavery agents, it was led by Theodore Weld, the movement's foremost organizer. There, under the impact of hearing the best abolitionist orators and activists report on their work, Sarah became converted to active abolitionism.

Weld, whose heroic feats of agitating for abolition and facing down mobs had become legendary, was a celebrated orator. He had over many years developed a biblical argument against slavery, and during the convention he spoke for four straight days on the topic. Angelina considered his speeches "a moral and intellectual feast," and Sarah was equally impressed.

Shortly after this convention Sarah wrote *An Epistle to the Clergy of the Southern States*, which was also published by the AASS. Weld did not write down his "Bible Argument" until after the convention, and it was published in 1837.[15] Although his work was published after Sarah's "Epistle," a comparison of the two pamphlets shows that she was influenced by him in important ways.

The core of Sarah's argument, that slavery is a crime because it converts man into a thing, a "chattel personal," is also central to Weld's "Bible argument." Both authors cite Genesis 26, "In the image of God created he them," and God's covenant with Noah (Gen. 9:3), in which he gives human beings dominion over animals and nature, as proof of God's intent of making a marked distinction between human beings and other creatures. Both authors assert that slavery tramples the image of God into dust and is therefore a sin. Sarah uses an interesting phrase here: ". . . we are fighting against God's unchangeable decree by depriving this rational and immortal being of those *inalienable rights* [emphasis mine] which have been conferred upon him" (p. 2). Her use of the language of the Bill of Rights foreshadows her later major contribution in bridging religious and political thought.

Grimké and Weld both cite Hebrew law against "man stealing." Both deny the slaveholders' assertion that the Bible sanctions slavery because of Noah's curse on Ham (Gen. 9:25). Sarah states simply that Canaan, not Ham, was the object of Noah's curse. Weld uses the same argument but elaborates by showing that Africans are not the descendants of Ham. Both Weld and Grimké make the point that Noah's statement regarding Ham is to be taken not as a curse but as a prophecy. It is a prophecy of what will happen to sinful humanity after the fall. The "prophecy" interpretation will be used again and quite powerfully by Sarah Grimké in her later work in reference to the curse on Eve.

The two Bible arguments differ greatly in elaboration and tone. Sarah cites the slave codes of several Southern states and uses anti-slavery statements made during the 1831 debate on slavery in the Virginia House of Delegates with great effectiveness.[16] Weld quotes from several of these speeches as well; he may, in this instance, have been influenced by her. Sarah also refers to recent events: the violence against antislavery speakers in the South, the burning of antislavery pamphlets in Charleston (among them Angelina's *Appeal*). She cites statements of Southern ministers in defense of slavery and expressions of outrage by Southeners in regard to the neglect of the religious training of slaves. Most interesting is her citation of a group of "Female citizens of Fluvanna County, Virginia," who in 1832 urged their representatives in the General Assembly of Virginia to listen "to the united voices of your mothers, wives, daughters and kindred" and consider slavery an evil (pp. 17–18).

The tone of the two works is quite different. Sarah uses biblical, prophetic language, keeping her tone exhortative and didactic. Weld speaks generally in a tone of learned detachment, using logical proof and examples. On occasion he departs from that tone to one of impassioned pleading or sharp satirical comment on proslavery arguments.

There is a difference also in the way both authors develop a philological argument. Weld argues that the word "buy" (as in "to buy a man") had vastly different meaning in biblical terms than in his day. In his *The Bible Against Slavery*, he also discusses other biblical words, such as the word *eber*, usually translated as "slave," which he claims should be "servant." This philological argument takes up several pages in his pamphlet. Weld compares linguistic usage in many different parts of the Bible, displays considerable learning and offers no apology nor does he cite other authorities for his interpretation.

Sarah confines her philological criticism to the translation of the word *eber* (servant/slave?). She cites a male authority, George M. Stroud, for the statement that the Hebrews had no word for "slave." "Had there been, as is asserted, slaves in Judea, there would undoubtedly have been some term to designate such a condition. Our language recognizes the difference between a slave and a servant, because those two classes actually exist in our country" (p. 7). Here her reasoning is straightforward, logical, and stated in plain language, but she cannot lay claim to erudition or expertise.

Her charge that the misogyny of the biblical text was due to deliberate misinterpretations in the translation of the Bible formed only a minor part of her argument in *Epistle*, but she would develop it into a much more important argument in her later work.

Sarah writes in the style of biblical prophesy, using highly charged and heavily metaphorical language. Some of it is quite trite, even banal. Much of it is exhortative: she is calling upon her sinful countrymen to repent and give up their sinful ways. "For you the midnight tear is shed, for you the daily and the nightly prayer ascends that God in his unbounded mercy may open your hearts to believe his awful enunciations against those who 'rob the poor because he is poor' " (p. 1). For the modern reader this makes for difficult reading.

In letters to friends written during the period of the writing of the *Epistle*, Sarah's style is quite different. She speaks in plain, everyday language, interspersed occasionally with a pious, prayerful stock phrase. She always wrote with a rather heavy hand and lacked the sprightly lucidity of Angelina's style, but her letters are practical, straightforward and lucid. Her style in the *Epistle* must be seen as a deliberate departure from her normal manner of thinking and speaking.

I have encountered this style many times over in different centuries in the writings of women mystics. It seems as though they were taking their vocabulary and sentence structure from the Bible, speaking in a voice that is not their own, but rather a voice laying claim to being "inspired." Some, like Mechthild of Magdeburg, never speak in a different voice; others, like Margery Kempe, Dorothea Montau and the seventeenth-century Pietists, mix both voices in their narrative, alternating between the ordinary woman with her ordinary speech and the inspired woman prophet. These stylistic choices were determined by the desperate social position of women intellectuals in their time—denied their full potential as thinking persons, castigated as intellectually inferior because of their gender, they felt the need to make themselves heard by speaking in a voice that distinguished them from the ordinary person, female or male. According to their religious indoctrination, woman could not speak— or write—for the public, but women inspired by God's gift of prophecy could aspire to such a public voice. Sarah Grimké, after her many years of humiliation and discouragement in her efforts to become a Quaker minister, assumed the voice of biblical prophecy for the same reason as had her predecessors—it was the only way she could imagine being heard.

Her *Epistle* repeatedly stresses her role as a Southerner, her intimate understanding of the actual workings of slavery, her sense of urgency over the sin of her countrymen, and, above all, the deeply-felt religious roots of her antislavery convictions. Compared with other antislavery appeals, such as William Lloyd Garrison's stirring *Address Delivered before the Free People of Color* (1831) or Lydia Maria Child's *Condition of Women in Various Ages*, it is neither particularly original nor rhetorically effective.[17] As is Angelina Grimké's *Appeal* to Southern women, it is distinguished by its Southern sensibilities and its emotional fervor. But in Sarah Grimké's growth as a a person and a thinker, it marks the end of a stage of her life. Never again would she write in the tone of prophecy; never again would she write in a voice so unlike her own. With the *Epistle* Sarah summed up the decades of her most strenuous and despairing religious struggles. Henceforth her visions and dreams were no longer calling her to a public role as a minister. By way of antislavery activism, Sarah would move to higher level of feminist consciousness and with it to independent thought.

The "parlour meetings" at which both sisters lectured in New York City were soon attended also by men; at a time when it was considered scandalous for respectable women to lecture in public, the fact of their lecturing to "mixed audiences" of men and women broke all precedent and contributed greatly to the sisters' fame in antislavery circles. The impact their lectures had made in New York City can be seen in the various offers proffered to them. Both were invited by Boston women to tour their area. Lecture invitations and the possibility of a teaching appointment for Angelina came from the President of Oberlin College. Sarah was invited to stay on in New York City and help with the drive for antislavery petitions and to "mingle with the people of color."[18]

As the sisters, together with other abolition women, prepared for the first convention of antislavery women, they concentrated their efforts on making the convention truly interracial. Sarah corresponded with her African-American friends in Philadelphia and urged them to attend the convention (see Article 18). She wrote to Anne Weston of the Boston Female Anti-Slavery Society:

> We hope to have the company of some of our colored sisters from your city; their voices will, we think, be needed. . . . I know of no

way so likely to destroy the cruel prejudices that exist as to bring our sisters in contact with those who shrink from such contact.[19]

The sisters had long befriended several black women in Philadelphia; they had visited their homes and had helped in supporting the Quaker-sponsored school for colored children. Now they moved into a more public assault on race prejudice. They formally asked their African-American friends to tell them of their personal experiences with race prejudice, possibly wanting to use the material at the convention.[20] When the Convention gathered in New York City in May 1837, both sisters were appointed officers, Sarah one of six Vice-Presidents, Angelina one of four secretaries.[21] The sisters' particular contribution was first, their mere presence as representatives of South Carolina, which is the way they identified themselves, and second, their insistence that, in order to abolish slavery, race prejudice must be fought in the North as well as in the South. Resolutions introduced by Angelina and approved by the Convention condemned the cooperation of North and South in supporting slavery; declared slavery a national sin; stated that the right of petition is inalienable. It was the duty and the province of women to petition for an end of slavery in D.C. and for abolition of the internal slave trade, and to plead the cause of the oppressed. One resolution declared: "The existence of an unnatural prejudice against our colored population is one of the chief pillars of American slavery," therefore we must "act out the principles of Christian equality by associating with them." Three other resolutions specified how to implement this support for interracial education.[22]

Sarah offered a resolution condemning "northern men and women, who marry slaveholders" because of their identification with a system "which desecrates the marriage relation among a large portion of the white inhabitants . . . and utterly destroys it among the victims of oppression." Another of her resolutions asked women on religious grounds "as moral and responsible beings" fully to discuss the subject of slavery. She endorsed "peace principles," and at her motion the convention endorsed the widespread circulation of antislavery prints (pictorial representations of the evils of slavery).

In these resolutions we see the development by both sisters of ideas they would later incorporate in their lectures and work: the emphasis on women as moral and responsible beings and therefore public citizens with rights and duties; the stress on race prejudice in the North as a support of the southern slave system; and the emphasis on petitioning as a political activity particularly suitable to women. The convention endorsed the last point with great emphasis by pledging to collect a million signatures on antislavery petitions.

The two formal publications endorsed and sponsored by this convention were written by the Grimké sisters—Angelina's *An Appeal to the Women of the Nominally Free States* and Sarah's *Address to Free Colored Americans.*[23] By the time the convention ended both sisters had become leaders of antislavery women.

Right after the convention the sisters undertook a lecture tour in New England (May-October 1837), which culminated in Angelina's testimony before the Massachusetts legislature in January 1838. The lecture tour is described in detail in my biography of the sisters. Its practical results in terms of organizational growth and petitioning activity are detailed in Article 19, below.

The first American woman ever to address a legislative body in behalf of other women, Angelina Grimké presented tens of thousands of antislavery petitions which had been collected by women. The tour was an organizational success which resulted not only in a mass petitioning campaign by women but also in the formation of dozens of female antislavery societies. In the course of their lecture tour, the sisters were attacked in the press and vilified from the pulpit. The Congregational clergy, which had long sought to silence antislavery speakers in the churches, on July 28, 1837, issued a "Pastoral Letter of the General Association of Massachusetts to the Congregational Churches under their care" which warned all churches against females "who so far forget themselves as to itinerate in the character of public lecturers and teachers" and exhorted women to "their appropriate duties" as stated in the New Testament. This attack on the only two women then publicly lecturing in New England, which was read from the pulpits in many churches and widely distributed, was part of an ongoing struggle within the New England churches over the issue of slavery and abolition and aimed, in its veiled attack on William Lloyd Garrison, to split the more conservative abolitionists from Garrison. Weld and the New York Anti-Slavery Society, which had for some time been highly critical of Garrison, sought to avoid further damage by playing down the controversy. Thus the sisters, inadvertently, got drawn into a leadership struggle within the abolition movement.

Faced with censure from the pulpit and in the press, they decided to defend the rights of women to a public voice in a series of essays written during their lecture tour, published first in antislavery newspapers and then as books (see below). To their dismay, far from defending them from these clerical attacks, male abolitionists, even Theodore Weld, pleaded with them not to take up the cause of women in public, lest they hurt the cause of the slave. Weld, who strongly believed in woman's right to lecture and to teach, argued, on pragmatic grounds, that at this time woman's rights should be subordinated to human rights. "Your womans rights! You put the cart before the horse . . . in attempting to push your *womans* rights, until human rights have gone ahead and broken the *path*," he wrote, following up this letter with several more in the same vein.[24]

Both sisters disagreed sharply with their mentor and advisor. "The time to assert a right, is *the time* when *that* right is denied," wrote Angelina. "*We must establish this right for if we do not, it will be impossible for* us to go on *with the work* of Emancipation."

"I do not feel as if I could surrender my right to discuss any great moral subject," Sarah stated. "If my connection with A.S. [Anti-Slavery Society] must continue at the expense of my conscience, I had far rather be thrown out of the A.S. ranks." And, as if to confirm her newly-found strength of purpose, she continued later: "I have written eight letters on the Province of woman. In the next two I shall take up the subject of the ministry of women."[25]

The rift between Weld and the sisters was soon settled amiably, and some months later he proposed marriage to Angelina and she accepted. Yet the incident was one of several which confirmed Sarah Grimké's feminism and strengthened her understanding of women's need to assert the autonomy of their minds.

The work Angelina produced during her lecture tour, *Letters to Catherine Beecher*, is a spirited defense of abolitionism and of women's moral responsibility to take a public stand on this issue. In ten of her thirteen letters Angelina developed her attack on colonization, her defense of immediate emancipation and her justification for the work of abolitionists. Her uncompromising attack on race prejudice as the chief support of the slave system reflected a stance she and Sarah had publicly advocated during the Female Anti-

Slavery Convention and which was their most original contribution
to antislavery thought.

Angelina used only two of her letters to respond to Catherine
Beecher's defense of "women's sphere" as purely domestic. By the
time she wrote these two letters, Sarah had nearly completed her
Letters on the Equality of the Sexes and the Condition of Women,
which had been published seriatim in *The New England Spectator*
and reprinted in William L. Garrison's abolitionist journal *The Liberator*. In Angelina's Letter XII she recommends this work for Catherine Beecher's perusal and states that it was "republished by Isaac
Knapp of Boston. As she [Sarah] has taken up this subject so fully,
I have only glanced at it." Angelina briefly summarizes the main
points of Sarah's more elaborate argument, in one case using the
same words Sarah used.[26] While the sisters undoubtedly developed
and discussed their ideas on women with each other, as they did on
most other subjects, it is Sarah who should be credited with developing the first comprehensive feminist argument presented by an
American woman, ten years before the Seneca Falls convention and
six years before the publication of Margaret Fuller's *Woman in the
Nineteenth Century*.[27]

The intellectual equipment Sarah Grimké brought to her task was
limited by her lack of formal education and by the ten years in which
her reading had been largely confined to material acceptable to Orthodox Quakers. She had a thorough knowledge of the biblical texts
in the King James version and had read and used several books of
commentaries. She had read Church history and some Quaker
texts.[28] It seems, at first, surprising that she was unacquainted with
the work of Margaret Fell, wife of George Fox, the founder of the
Society of Friends. Margaret Fell (1614–1702), while serving a
prison sentence for advocating her religious beliefs, wrote *Women's
Speaking Justified*, a fully developed scriptural argument justifying
women's right to participate in public religious life and thought.[29]
Citing chapter and verse in both Old and New Testament, listing
every woman who had prophesied, spoken or acted, and reinter-
preting the core Bible passage used to justify misogyny, she had done
in 1667 the work Sarah set out to do in 1837. But, in a manner
typical for the writings of women throughout history, Fell's pamphlet was printed once, and until the twentieth century it was not
reprinted in the United States. Thus, Sarah could begin her essay by

stating: "I feel that I am venturing on nearly untrodden ground," thereby acting out a basic principle of women's subordination—that intellectual women were destined to reinvent the wheel over and over again. She was equally ignorant of the literally dozens of feminist Bible critics who had preceded her. Thus, her work was wholly original, even though now, after the at least partial restoration of women's history, we know that it is in fact part of a long tradition.

She had read Locke, Jefferson, and probably others of the founding fathers, and was, through conversations with her father and her brothers, well acquainted with the rights ideology of the Enlightenment and of the American Revolution. Exposure to the antislavery writings and speeches of Garrison, James Birney and Weld had made her knowledgeable about the major ideas of abolitionist thinkers and evangelical reformers. Recently under the influence of the utopian perfectionist Henry C. Wright, she had absorbed "ultra" peace and anarchistic ideas. But she approached this work from the stance of a sectarian of the radical left wing of the Protestant Reformation, insisting on her right to interpret the text for herself.

She ascribed all misogynist writings based on biblical texts to

> misconception of the simple truths revealed in the Scriptures, in consequence of the false translation of many passages of Holy Writ.
> . . . My mind is entirely delivered from the superstitious reverence which is attached to the English version of the Bible. King James's translators certainly were not inspired. I therefore claim the original as my standard, *believing that to have been inspired,* and I also claim to judge for myself what is the meaning of the inspired writers . . . and not be governed by the views of any man, or set of men.

She reinforced her "translation" argument later in Letter III:

> I am inclined to think, when we [women] are admitted to the honor of studying Greek and Hebrew, we shall produce some various readings of the Bible a little different from those we now have.[30]

Reiterating her Protestant insistence on the right of each individual to interpret the scriptures, she ended the first letter with the phrase: "Here then I plant myself. God created us equal," echoing Luther's statement before the Diet of Worms in 1521.[31]

She stressed the equal creation of man and woman ("male and female created He them") and the fact that, despite the existence of many animals, God wanted Adam to have a companion *"in all re-spects* his equal; one who was like himself *a free agent,* gifted with intellect and endowed with immortality." She pointed out that the word "Adam" is "a generic term, including man and woman," an observation quite original in her day.[32]

She considered Adam and Eve equally guilty in the Fall: "They both fell from innocence, and consequently from happiness, *but not from equality,"* an interpretation made before her by Isotta Nogarola (1418–66), Rachel Speght (1600?–?), Aemilia Lanyer (1569–1645), among others. But Sarah did not know of their existence or their work. Her interpretation of God's so-called "curse on Eve" was innovative. She argued that

> the curse . . . is simple prophecy. The Hebrew, like our French language, uses the same word to express shall and will. Our translators having been accustomed to exercise lordship over their wives, and seeing only through the medium of perverted judgement . . . translated it *shall* instead of *will,* and thus converted a prediction to Eve into a command to Adam.[33]

Grimké's reference to the "perverted judgement" of the translators echoes her comments on the mistranslations of words relating to servitude in *Epistle,* only now her observation that translators are influenced by the thought and concepts current during their time has a feminist tinge. Male translators have shown bad faith by imposing their views of gender on the text, she charged. She continued to pursue the theme of male intellectual dominance in the later work, charging that man had exercised "dominion" over women "for nearly six thousand years."

> All history attests that man has subjected woman to his will, used her as a means to promote his selfish gratification, to minister to his sensual pleasures, to be instrumental in promoting his comfort; but never has he desired to elevate her to that rank she was created to fill. He has done all he could to debase and enslave her mind; and now he looks triumphantly on the ruin he has wrought, and says, the being he has thus deeply injured is his inferior.[34]

Here is the core of Sarah's feminist argument, and with it she advances far beyond any of her predecessors and her contemporaries. The charge that men have used women, instrumentalized them, and benefitted from their subordination advances feminist thought decisively over the Enlightenment argument in which women's inalienable rights are asserted. Grounding her theory in her personal experience, Sarah was able to connect the theory of rights and the moral argument based on religious considerations with a social analysis that took power into account. Other feminist thinkers before her had shown that women had suffered a wrong or wrongs; many others had asserted woman's moral and spiritual equality; but Sarah took the step into social analysis by showing that wherever power is exercised over a group of people someone benefits and someone is exploited. She had learned this from living within the slave system; now she made the intellectual leap of reasoning from the power/oppression model of slavery to the power/oppression of woman. This is quite different from the use of the metaphor of "white woman" as sister to the slave woman, which was often used by abolitionists and has recently been the focus of much attention by contemporary analysts.[35]

Sarah Grimké here managed to construct social theory on the basis of comparing two kinds of systems of oppression. She never made the mistake of equating the white woman's position with that of the slave, and she always emphasized the greater suffering, exploitation and oppression of the black woman. But her description of the process by which the deprivation of women is reinforced by prejudice and justified by observing the very results of that deprivation applies with equal force to the victims of racism.

In a refutation of the arguments made in the "Pastoral Letter of the Congregational Churches," Sarah challenged the pervasive "doctrine of [woman's] dependence on man," by which he has sought to corrupt women's spirit by flattery, "baubles and geegaws," and to make her "satisfied with the privileges which man has assumed to grant her." As for the injunction that women must be instructed in religious matters by their ministers, she answered scathingly: "Now this is assuming that all pastors are better qualified to give instruction than woman. This I utterly deny. I have suffered too keenly from the teaching of man, to lead anyone to him for instruction."[36]

Sarah defined and explored the concept "gender" without using the word. "Nothing, I believe, has tended more to destroy the true dignity of woman, than the fact that she is approached by man in the character of a female." (She uses the term "female" to describe the gendered creature created by man, in contrast to the divinely created "woman.") And again, in a later section:

> [I]ntellect is not sexed . . . strength of mind is not sexed; and . . . our views about the duties of men and the duties of women, the sphere of man and the sphere of woman, are mere abitrary opinions, differing in different ages and countries, and dependant solely on the will and judgement of erring mortals.[37]

Here, relying only on her own judgment and interpretations, Sarah defined the difference between sex and gender in terms which would not be as clearly stated again until the 20th century. Gender is a culturally variable, arbitrary definition of behavior deemed appropriate to each of the sexes in different ages and places.

Man, she charges, addresses himself to the weakness of woman instead of uplifting her. Once he has gained her affections, "he furnishes himself with a housekeeper, whose chief business is the kitchen, or the nursery."[38] He pursues his economic and intellectual interests, while condemning her to isolation within the home.

Discussing the rights of women to teach, she asks why ministers, who stand firm against women's preaching, still employ women as Sunday school teachers.

> Simply . . . because in the one case we subserve [serve] *their* views and *their interests,* and act in subordination to them; whilst in the other, we come in contact with [contradict] their interests, and claim to be on an equality with them in . . . the ministry of the word.[39]

In three of her letters (5, 6, 7) Sarah critically surveyed women's condition in different cultures at various times. Her survey of women's status in Asia and Africa and in Western civilization leans heavily on the work of Lydia Maria Child.[40] It is infused with the conviction that women fared far worse under "heathenism" than under Christianity. She accepted uncritically and unquestioningly the interpretation of her male sources which held Jews responsible for oppressing women and denying them rights, whereas Christianity exerted a "genial influence" on the condition of women.[41]

Sarah Grimké, following a centuries-old tradition among feminist thinkers, provided a comprehensive list of women of achievement, prophets and ministers, heroic and learned women. This rudimentary effort at constructing "Women's History" was designed to provide proof that women were not and never had been inferior to men. But Sarah did not stop there. In constructing her argument, she anticipated by dozens of years the main points advocates of woman's rights would make for the next century. She blamed inferior education given women and their lack of economic choices outside of marriage for many of women's defects and disabilities. She even demanded equal pay for equal work and wrote with rare understanding about the low wages paid to women workers. Urging women to become conscious of their own dignity and worth, she ridiculed the practice of having male ministers open the meetings of women's organizations and advised women, who in sewing circles raised money to supply the needs of ministerial students, to work for the advancement of their own sex instead.

She surveyed the laws which worked to the detriment of women and concluded: "Woman has no political existence. With the single exception of presenting a petition to the legislative body, she is a cipher in the nation." She considered the legal disabilities of married women an abuse of power by men and demanded equality under the law and rights of citizenship for women.

While she echoed Mary Wollstonecraft's argument that the elevation of women would benefit men by their having more enlightened wives and companions, Sarah Grimké moved far ahead of that view in a woman-centered direction. Women "really are, FREE AGENTS, immortal beings." They needed to grasp the privileges and advantages which were within their reach, become conscious of their rights as moral beings. And with a message which is several times repeated in her essay, she summed up her feminist argument, which combined religious and natural rights principles:

WHATSOEVER IT IS MORALLY RIGHT FOR A MAN TO DO, IT IS MORALLY RIGHT FOR A WOMAN TO DO ... she is clothed by her Maker with the *same rights*, and ... the *same duties*.[42]

Letters on the Equality of the Sexes marks Sarah Grimké as a major theorist and pioneer of feminism. Her contemporaries understood the significance of her work. Lucy Stone called it "first rate" and said it confirmed her resolution "to call no man master." Abby Kelley and Elizabeth Cady Stanton acknowledged the impact of her work on their own development. Lucretia Mott called the book the most important work since Mary Wollstonecraft's *Rights of Women*.[43] Yet the work has been neglected and forgotten until recently, when it was republished. It is now available in several editions, which is why it is not included in this volume.[44]

The sisters' New England speaking tour ended in 1838, shortly followed by Angelina's marriage to Theodore Weld. The couple and Sarah Grimké, who made her home with them, moved to a small farm in Raritan Bay, N.J. The three collaborated on a documentary pamphlet, a searing indictment of slavery, *American Slavery As It Is: Testimony of a Thousand Witnesses* (1839), which was the most important antislavery publication before *Uncle Tom's Cabin*, for which it served as one source.[45] Sarah's contribution to the book was to recount every memory of brutality against slaves she had personally witnessed in Charleston. The accounts are harrowing. Told in plain, factual language quite different from Sarah's usual writing style, they contrast the mistreatment given the slaves with the high social standing and gentility of the planters and their wives. What Sarah illustrates most vividly is the "banality of evil," its commonplace nature and the societal acceptance of atrocities against black people which would never be tolerated against whites. But she also shows unblinkingly the brutality perpetrated by slaveholding women against their victims. Describing the plight of a young runaway slave woman, who was severely whipped, had an iron collar placed upon her neck and a sound front tooth extracted for easier identification, Sarah commented:

> These outrages were committed in a family where the mistress daily read the scriptures. . . . She was accounted, and was really, so far as almsgiving was concerned, a charitable woman, and tender hearted to the poor; and yet this suffering slave, who was the seamstress of the family, was continually in her presence, sitting in her chamber to sew . . . with her lacerated and bleeding back, her mutilated mouth, and heavy iron collar, without, so far as appeared, exciting any feelings of compassion.[46]

American Slavery As It Is, printed in 1839, sold over 100,000 copies in the first year and was widely read and distributed also in Great Britain. It had been a physically and emotionally exhausting work to which the sisters had contributed not only their own reminiscences, but six months of intense research and editing. It was the last sustained intellectual work they were able to do for a long time.

In December 1839 Angelina gave birth to her first child, a boy, in an uneventful birth, but she contracted mastitis and was seriously ill for weeks. Then, shortly after the birth and probably too soon for the mother's comfort, the family moved to larger quarters, a farm in Belleville, N.J.

Theodore Weld, a dedicated idealist and reformer, never made an adequate living for his family. His antislavery activities caused him to be frequently absent from home, so that he could only intermittently attend to his farm. Angelina gave birth to another son in 1841 and to a daughter in 1844. She had a miscarriage between the first and the second pregnancy, while her husband was in Washington running an antislavery research bureau. She was in ill health after her last pregnancy, suffering from a prolapsed uterus and an untreated hernia, conditions which are surgically treatable today, but which were incurable in the mid nineteenth century and which caused her at times excruciating pain and serious discomfort for the rest of her life. In the crucial years when Angelina was weakened by the physical disabilities resulting from child-bearing, the burden of household and child care fell to Sarah. It was then she became a surrogate mother for Angelina's children, a situation which Angelina not only tolerated but often encouraged. This kind of domestic arrangement was not at all unusual in mid-nineteenth century. Raising the Welds' three children, struggling under severe economic constraints, the sisters were unable and unwilling to continue their public speaking careers. Both sisters continued their interest in antislavery and woman's rights, but Sarah never again spoke in public. It was not until the Civil War that Angelina again took an active part in a woman's organization. In 1863 she gave her last public lecture at the Convention of the Woman's National Loyal League.

In my biography of the Grimké sisters I traced the conflicting demands and interests that caused the Weld household to develop as it did. From 1848 on Weld and the sisters ran a boarding school on their New Jersey farm. But the school failed to support the family adequately. When in 1852 an invitation came to Theodore Weld to join the newly formed Raritan Bay Union community and take charge of its school, the family seriously considered this move. The offer was generous in that Weld would have full control of the school and Sarah and Angelina would be employed as teachers. Raritan Bay Union was an offspring of the Fourierist North American Phalanx at Red Bank, N.J., a utopian community which had been fairly prosperous for eleven years. Thirty dissident members now planned to secede and form their own agrarian settlement, which would be run on communal principles but with a more strongly religious and educational orientation. Communitarian living greatly appealed to Weld, and Angelina looked forward to seeing her husband in a prestigious educational role and herself as a teacher, rather than as boarding-school keeper. But Sarah had great hesitations about joining a utopian community; she feared losing privacy and she did not want to continue working as a teacher. The impending decision produced a profound crisis in her life, which was aggravated by a bitter confrontation between the sisters over a problem they had suppressed for nearly fifteen years—the conflict over Sarah's role as surrogate mother of the Weld children.

After the early childhood years of her children had passed, Angelina began to fret over the dominant role Sarah had assumed in the family. She suppressed her feelings and blamed herself for not sharing her blessings fully enough with her sister. But there was also the matter of her family's partial dependence on Sarah's money. This must have happened quite gradually, with little gifts or loans on Sarah's part, when she noticed a need in the household. Now Angelina looked to the family's move as a chance to improve their earnings. She hoped, after the sale of the Belleville farm, to repay Sarah for her investments in the household and to separate her and Sarah's monetary affairs.[47] Sarah took this suggestion badly; she chose to regard it as a rebuff not only of her money but of herself. She considered striking out on her own and starting an independent life. Angelina encouraged her to leave.

Sarah wrote her friend Harriot Hunt that she would love to spend a winter in Boston and wanted to attend Margaret Fuller's "Conversations." What held her back was her attachment to Angelina's children.

A separation from these darling children who have brightened a few years of my lonely and sorrowful life, over whelmed me, when I first

thought of it as the probable result of the contemplated change. I
turned from it in deep anguish. . . . They seemed to be the link that
bound me to life . . . without them existence would have no charms.—
I know this appears extravagant, but it is true. . . . Gradually I can
look at this separation with some calmness.[48]

There is no question that Sarah's emotional attachment to the
children was excessive and unrestrained. She, too, like most women
of her generation, had since early childhood been schooled in sup-
pressing her feelings and expressing anger only through self-blame.
From her point of view, she had been sacrificing her mind and energy to becoming a household drudge and surrogate mother, in order to help her younger sister during illness and periods of stress.
Sarah never gave up her role as Angelina's mother. Angelina, who
had struggled against her slaveholder mother by leaving her and the
South, could never escape that other mothering. The conflict the
sisters expressed for the first time overtly during this period had
complex roots; it had elements of a generational conflict mixed with
sibling rivalry and the inevitable domestic conflicts deriving from
overwork, ill health and poverty. The fact is, in 1852, both sisters
felt disappointed, trapped and resentful, and chafed against the restraints placed on their ability to think and work for the political
causes in which they so fervently believed.[49]

Sarah, at age sixty, explored the possibility of getting professional
training as a doctor or a lawyer. "There is plenty of work to be
done, but I see nothing in the wide world that I can do," she cried
out in despair.

[T]he powers of my mind have never been allowed expansion; in
childhood they were repressed by the false idea that a girl need not
have the education I coveted. In early youth by wrong views of God
and religion, then I was fairly ground to powder in the Quaker Society and have been ever since . . . by the overwhelming superiority
of those with whom I have been in contact. Now, after all what can
I expect in old age?[50]

All her inquiries resulted in disappointment. The study of law was
still closed to women; the study of medicine was unthinkable for a
woman her age. She then began to work on a compilation of laws

pertaining to women in order to expose their unfairness. A number of essay fragments found in her papers, which cannot be precisely dated, were probably written during this period. She may have intended them as a sequel to her first book. At any rate, her search for independence soon ended. After a stay of a few months first in Boston, then in Washington, D.C., Sarah responded to her sister's plea to come home by returning to the Weld household, where she spent the rest of her life.

In the Fourierist cooperative community at Raritan Bay, N.J., Weld became the director of the school, which he developed into one of the pioneering educational establishments of the time. Weld attracted an outstanding teaching staff and ran a coeducational, interracial school which combined manual labor with classical training, art education, drama and physical education. Both sisters taught school the rest of their lives, but the occupation was not intellectually satisfying to Sarah.

In the last decade of her life, she was increasingly preoccupied with metaphysical manifestations and dreams she considered prophetic. She experienced visits and conversations with the dead. Her mother, and sometimes her father and brother, appeared to her to guide her in making decisions. Her attraction to organized Spiritualism revived her mystical tendencies and, as earlier in her life, helped her in a period of spiritual and mental disappointments. Spiritualists had fully embraced the equality of women and acknowledged women's gift for the ministry. Sarah Grimké was only one of many of the most advanced radical thinkers of her day to be attracted to Spiritualism.[51]

The essay fragments written in the seventh decade of her life represent Sarah Grimké's final intellectual contribution. They are, on the whole, more radical than anything she wrote earlier. I shall discuss them here in what I believe to be their chronological order.

Sarah's longest essay, "The Education of Women" (Doc. 8), marks her farthest movement away from a largely moral and religious conceptual framework. Grounding her argument in a theory of history in which change is the engine of progress and knowledge "the lever which has raised man to a higher state," she argues for giving women equal access to education. Citing examples from his-

tory of the achievements of educated "heathen" women, she con-
trasts their situation with the dismal situation of Christian women
denied access to knowledge.

Sarah takes the unusual step of including in her essay the story of
her own struggles for education and of her sufferings because she
was denied it. "I believe that my sorrows are not uncommon sorrows," she explained. ". . . Many a woman shudders as she takes a
retrospect of life at the terrible eclipse of those intellectual powers,
which in early life seemed prophetic of usefulness and happiness."[52]

Education must equip women for economic independence and for
social usefulness. This recurrent theme is elaborated here and reinforced by the sharpest critique of male prerogative in her work:

> Let us redeem ourselves from the degradation which has been the
> natural consequence of woman's having been regarded a mere instru-
> ment to be used for the gratification of passion, as the upper servant
> in the domestic relations of man to keep things comfortable for her
> lord, to prepare . . . his food and clothing to produce a pair of slippers
> to put on . . . and to nurse *his* babies. I may not say *hers*, for too
> often she has not been a willing partner to their birth. . . .
>
>   It is because we feel this so keenly that we now demand an equal
> education with man. It is because we feel that we have powers which
> are crushed, responsibilities which we are not permitted to exercise
> . . . rights vested in us as moral and intellectual beings, which are
> utterly ignored and trampled upon. It is because we feel this so keenly
> that we now demand an equal education with man. . . . [53]

Another unfinished essay, preserved only in several notebooks, is
entitled "Marriage." In the summer of 1855 a *New York Times*
essayist declared that the woman's movement "directly and rapidly"
leads toward "Free Love." Sarah Grimké challenged this view in her
essay. She forcefully denied the essayist's assertion that giving
woman "complete sovereignty over her own person and conduct"
would nullify the marriage relationship. It would, on the contrary,
"purify and exalt the marriage relation and destroy *all* licentiousness."[54]

The evils of the current marriage system are caused by man's usurpation of power over woman and by man's licentious nature. Using
language which in her day would have been considered utterly
shocking, Sarah focused on what today we call "marital rape" as

the source of women's unhappiness, her ill health caused by too frequent pregnancies and the sickliness of many children.

> Oh, how many women who have entered the marriage relation in all purity and innocence, expecting to realize in it the completion of their own halfness, the rounding out of their own being . . . have too soon discovered that they were unpaid housekeepers and nurses, and still worse, chattels permanent to be used and abused at the will of a master. . . . How many so-called wives, rise in the morning oppressed with a sense of degradation from the fact that their chastity has been violated . . . themselves humbled [by] a so called husband [who] has been the perpetrator of the unnatural crime.[55]

Social causes are at the root of the unhappiness of so many families. Sarah lists these as ignorance of physical facts "which every man and woman ought to know before marriage"; false notions of man's physical needs; the fact that many marriages are not love marriages. She paints a touching, idealized picture of loving unions, based on recognition of the "divinity of mind and soul." The purest and most unselfish love is "the spontaneous giving away of oneself to the only loved one and the receiving of that other to ourselves in return." While she advocates woman's absolute right to control the frequency of sexual intercourse, she concedes that such intercourse may continue even after the childbearing period is over, as long as it as an expression of love and respect.

"Men must grow out of that non-development in which they now are" and women must have equality of rights. But this will not happen until her education improves so that she can gain that "pecuniary independence which would lift her above the temptation to marry for a home."[56] Here she expresses the linkage between woman's sexual subordination and her economic dependency, an idea which seemed radical even a hundred years later.

The essay reflects the views on sexual purity held by many reformers of her day and repeats some of the misconceptions which were then prevalent about "loss of seminal fluid" and its dire consequences for the mind. Sarah's accomplishment is to tie these ideas together in a coherent feminist argument, in which economic and political rights are seen as the necessary precondition for winning sexual rights and what today we would call a woman's "right to her own body."

In 1857, in a letter to her friend Harriot Hunt, Sarah writes that she has just completed a "homespun essay on the Query 'Ought Woman to have the elective franchise?' " and is trying to get it published. Only a fragment of this essay survives in her papers. One may assume it served as a draft for most of the ideas she expressed in her essay "The Education of Women."[57]

Sarah had for several years been working on a compilation of the laws relating to women, hoping to publish a book on the subject. Nothing ever came of that project, except a few scattered notes and a brief unpublished "Essay on the Laws Respecting Women." In it she reiterates her peace principles and refers appreciatively to Florence Nightingale's work of establishing schools for nursing. She also restates her argument for woman's equality with an appeal to Enlightenment thought: it is woman's reason "that rouses her to an effort to obtain a repeal of the unrighteous laws which . . . mortify and dwindle her."[58]

She elaborated on her legal argument in a series of "Lecture Notes."

> The state ought not to interfere with the Liberty of any of its subjects. . . . It is bound to provide for all men equal access to the existing sources of the culture . . . and that is only possible by the establishment of an absolute equality in personal as well as civil freedom in rights. . . . The time has arrived when woman may justly claim her rights, when she may freely own to have a share in the enactment & administration of the laws by wh[ich] she is governed.[59]

Sarah continued her argument for women's legal rights in "Sisters of Charity." That lengthy essay, together with "The Education of Women," represents the most complete and mature expression of her feminist thought. The first essay was written in the form of commentaries on a book she had evidently just read, Anna Jameson's *Sisters of Charity* . . . (1855).[60] Sarah added to Jameson's vigorous attack on laws that discriminate against women quotations from the report of a volunteer nurse working with Florence Nightingale in the Crimea in order to strengthen her argument for enlarging "woman's sphere." She improved upon Jameson's argument by showing how discrimination and women's exclusion from participation in economic and political life had affected them psychologically: "At present women are depressed by the laws, depressed by a public opinion resulting from the laws, depressed by the prejudice of parents and guardians, till the great part of the sex is ignorant of its powers."[61]

"The laws respecting married women are one of the greatest outrages that has been perpetrated against God and humanity," Sarah charged, which foster "on the one side injustice and oppression and on the other . . . loss of self-respect, independence and degradation." She demanded that women be taught "self-respect and self-reliance by giving her just and equal laws." Her impassioned outcry goes far beyond Jameson's moderate proposal for liberal reforms. Grimké expresses both anguish and anger and sees the antagonists as separate classes:

> It is self evident that inequality of rights creates antagonism and the assumption that we must continue in this state is productive of nothing but evil, because the privileged and the oppressed stand in opposition to each other, the latter yielding unwillingly the distinctions which the former demand and the former shutting themselves up in the self made circle of their superiority. . . . How shall these two classes harmonize?[62]

In these essays Sarah expresses an understanding of class which is highly unusual among antebellum reformers. She repeatedly makes references to the plight of working women, of needle trades workers, of women kept out of skilled occupations. She demands equal pay for equal work and equal access to training opportunities. She even offers a rudimentary class theory: "It is not from women who are reclining in the lap of opulence and splendor, and eating the bread of idleness, that we can expect aid. . . . Reformers have almost universally arisen among what are termed the inferior classes of society. . . . Those who feel the daily calamity of unjust laws . . . , whose souls are on fire because of oppression . . . these are the men and women who awaken public attention to the needed reformation."[63]

Sarah's understanding of economic forces was based entirely on her own life experience. Ever since she had left South Carolina, she had been living a life of respectable poverty. The small income from her inheritance might have been sufficient to provide her with middle class comfort, but Weld's precarious economic position as a paid organizer of the always poverty-stricken AASS meant that the family depended heavily on Sarah's financial contributions. When, in 1853, she contemplated living independently, the implications of her highly limited choices as a self-supporting woman sharpened her thinking on the subject of class.[64] Sarah Grimké was undoubtedly familiar with the sharply polarized version of the relations of the sexes expressed in the "Declaration of Sentiments" of the 1848 Seneca Falls Convention and the more self-consciously feminist resolutions of the 1850 Ohio Woman's Rights Convention. These are reflected in her writings in the unpublished essays. But the strong emphasis throughout her notes on the need to develop women's feminist consciousness is her own.

She believed not only in the existence of a separate woman's sphere but in the superiority and uniqueness of "woman's culture." And she reflected the stages of her own developing sense of autonomy and selfhood in a passage which anticipated by nearly forty years the ideas to which Elizabeth Cady Stanton would give wide currency in her most celebrated speech, the "Solitude of Self" lecture.

> Thus far woman has struggled through life with bandaged eyes, accepting the dogma of her weakness and inability to take care of herself not only physically but intellectually. She has held out a trembling hand and received gratefully the proffered aid. She has foregone her right to study, to know the laws and purposes of government to which she is subject. But now there is awakened in her a consciousness that she is defrauded of her legitimate Rights and that she never can fulfill her mission until she is placed in that position to which she feels herself called by the divinity within. Hitherto she has surrendered her person and her individuality to man, but she can no longer do this and not feel that she is outraging her nature and her God. There is now predominant in the minds of intelligent women to an extent never known before a struggling after freedom, an intense desire after a higher life. . . . Self reliance only can create true and exalted women."[65]

Sarah's proposed remedy for the profound injustices under which women labored was simple: " 'Establish Justice' which will insure 'domestic tranquility, promote the general welfare and secure the blessings of liberty' to women and to posterity" (p. 144 below). Here Sarah roots her claim to woman's rights once again in the ideology of the American Constitution and the Declaration of Independence. But she goes further and castigates "the horrors of forced maternity"—a euphemism for marital rape—as one of the primary evils which equal rights legislation would have to address. These ideas, which she had earlier expressed in her essay "Marriage," put Sarah Grimké far ahead of her contemporaries. An analysis that put emphasis on woman's sexual subordination had characterized the thinking of the Owenite wing of British reform in the 1830s and 40s. It came to the United States in the person and writings of Frances Wright. Ideas linking women's emancipation with sexual emancipation were also expressed by French and British Saint-Simonians in the aftermath of the 1848 revolutions. They came to the United States through communications from foreign feminists to the various woman's rights conventions in the 1850s. Sarah Grimké was acquainted with these and with the writings of Harriet Taylor and John Stuart Mill (see p. 40 below). Historians have assumed that antebellum feminist thought was quite untouched by this type of analysis until the 1870s, when Elizabeth Cady Stanton publicly stated her unorthodox ideas on woman's sexual oppression. The Sarah Grimké essays point us to an earlier occurrence of this line of reasoning on American soil.[66]

In her unpublished essays Sarah Grimké advanced her analysis of women's situation over that which she had given in *Letters* by blending her religious argument with natural rights theory and with a radical theory concerning woman's sexual oppression. She integrated much of the wide reading she had done in history and even the sciences to reason with far more complexity than in her earlier work.

In her sixties, Sarah Grimké attempted, as best she could, to keep up with feminist ideas generated at home and abroad. She read and greatly admired Elizabeth Barrett Browning's *Aurora Leigh*, a work which served as inspiration to many American feminists. She recommended the book to her friends, even before she had read it, as described in the following letter to her young friends in Kansas, Augustus and Sarah Wattles:

Have you received Aurora Leigh [?] I have not yet read it, but feel sure that it will amply reward you for the time you bestow upon it.

The first epic written by a woman it is a grand effort of intellect and heart. Such portraitures of woman as she may be, as she will be, as some few of us now are, cannot fail to stir up within us the elements of progress and carry us forward on the tide of improvement."[67]

Her interest in the work of feminists in other countries even included the fine arts. She reported to the Wattleses on a marvelous exhibition in New York City: "A painting of horses half as large as life [,] said to be the finest effort of art in that line the world has ever seen by Rosa Bonner."[68] Undoubtedly, she meant a painting by the French artist Rosa Bonheur, which she evidently had not seen herself but which she celebrated because it was the work of a woman.

She read Charlotte Brontë's *Villette*, Victor Hugo's *Les Misérables,* and the speeches of the Hungarian revolutionary Louis Kossuth. Her familiarity with the work of contemporary British feminists is evident in her references to the writings of Florence Nightingale and Anna Jameson. Her letter to Jeanne Deroin, with its references to Deroin's feminist publication, shows how closely she felt her connection to feminists in other countries. In the years when her desire for a professional education had finally and irrevocably been crushed, she responded by doing a translation of Lamartine's biography of Jeanne d'Arc, which was published in the United States in 1867.

Sarah Grimké was familiar with the works and the autobiography of George Sand. In one of her notebooks filled with citations there are four pages of quotations in French by George Sand, regarding marriage. There is also a quotation from the author's autobiography: "If we seek repose in the absence of sorrow, of fatigue of anxiety [*sic*] we shall plunge ourselves into a state of insensibility, imbecility, anticipated death. *Quand on accepte un mal incurable, on le support mieux.*"

A draft of her letter to George Sand, written in English, is among Sarah Grimké's papers (see Doc. 16). Its naive assumption that the great author would be willing to assist her in finding a picture of Jeanne d'Arc speaks to Sarah's sense of "sisterhood." She would have gladly honored any request for help or information from a foreign feminist, yet she was aware that the famous author might regard her request as an imposition.

In 1854 Sarah said in a letter that she no longer believed slavery could be peacefully abolished in the United States (see Doc. 6). She followed the events in Kansas closely, sympathizing with and fearing for her friends, the Wattleses. By 1856 her "ultra" peace principles had crumbled under the neccessity of events. Regarding the late news from Kansas she wrote to Sarah Wattles:

> This country has made herself drunk with the blood of the victims of oppression and she must reap the fruit of her doings. Yes, liberty must have her martyrs. A truer and higher liberty than was fought for by our revolutionary fathers is now calling forth the energies of abolitionists, and though the result of the struggle must be freedom for the colored man, fraternity for the race, yet a time I fear awaits us that will try men's souls . . . [69]

The Welds, Sarah and most of the old abolitionists endorsed the Civil War because they saw it as the final battle to end slavery. They had little confidence in President Lincoln and criticized him for fighting the war for the Union but not for abolition. Sarah expressed her political critique eloquently and shrewdly, sometime late during the war:

> Until this nation is willing to accept the colored man as a brother, to acknowledge him as an American, to place him on the same footing as the descendants of any other nation—they cannot fulfill their destiny, they cannot conquer in this fearful struggle. The slaves hold the balance of victory in their hands, God grant, we may meet reverses until sufferings bring repentance, and repentance a recognition that all men are brethren, and that "life, liberty and the pursuit of happiness["] is the God given right of all. When I hear of our successes I feel no elation, when I hear of our defeats I welcome the chastisement as a mark of divine love, because there is a deep conviction that nothing will bring this nation to do justice, but bitter agony. The measure we have meted out to others in severing the tenderest ties of nature, in wantonly inflicting wounds and bruises and putrefying sores upon the prostrate slave, is being measured to us again in our hospitals and on our battlefields. All is working together for the deliverance of the captive. Who has a right to fight this battle for freedom if not the slave. He will fight it and have a claim to our honor and our gratitude . . . [70]

Her understanding of the need to fight racism was as strong as ever. Her sense of righteousness and moral strength was undimmed.

As always, she saw the struggle against slavery as a religious battle between good and evil. The sinful nation had to purge itself before it could be free of prejudice. "Nothing will bring this nation to justice, but bitter agony." Unblinkingly, Sarah Grimké looked at the future and foresaw that the end of the Civil War would not bring the end of racism.

But she never lost her courage and her dedication to the dissemination of progressive ideas. At the age of seventy-seven, Sarah Grimké trudged up and down the Massachusetts countryside, selling 150 copies of John Stuart Mill's *The Subjection of Women* and circulating woman's suffrage petitions.[71]

Late in life, after discovering the existence of two black nephews, sons of their brother Henry and one of his slaves, the sisters adopted the young men into their family and helped finance their education. In March 1870, the sisters, together with forty other women, participated in a suffrage demonstration by marching to the polls in a howling snowstorm and depositing their ballots in a special receptacle the election officials had designated for the purpose. It was a small, defiant gesture of no immediate significance. It would take fifty more years of nationwide organizing and agitating before women would gain the vote. The sisters' organizing and public speaking had paved the way for future generations of activists.

Sarah Grimké's feminist thought had leaped far ahead of her generation, even her century. Seen in the light of twentieth-century feminist theory her accomplishment is remarkable: She offered the best and most coherent Bible argument for woman's equality yet offered by a woman; she identified and characterized the distinction between sex and gender; she took class and race into consideration; and she tied the subordination of women both to educational deprivation and sexual oppression. She identified men, individually and as a group, as having benefitted from the subordination of women. Above all, she understood that women must acquire feminist consciousness by conscious effort and that they must practice asserting their rights in order to think more appropriately. Using her own life as an example, she showed that the personal experience is rooted in social reality.

This remarkable achievement ended in disappointment and failure, as did the achievement of so many talented thinking women of the past. The essays were not published, the *Letters* disappeared after one edition. Sarah had no sense of her own achievement. The single biography written about her and Angelina in the nineteenth century was written by a friend and contemporary, Catherine Birney, and published in 1883. Neither sister was mentioned in the historiography of antislavery until 1961, when Dwight L. Dumond, the historian who discovered the Weld papers, dedicated a chapter in his book to them and described the outlines of their antislavery work. My biography of the Grimké sisters in 1967 was the first book-length biography of them since Birney's. And, as I stated earlier, more recent historiography of the sisters has not sufficiently done justice to Sarah Grimké's work and ideas.

That her ideas came to us in snippets and fragments, handwritten on paper cut out of a notebook, embedded in the manuscript collection of her brother-in-law, unnoticed in her day and forgotten for over a hundred years is typical of what happened to the intellectual work of women. Her vision has yet to become fully realized, but, at long last, we may honor her as a major feminist thinker.

NOTES

1. Gerda Lerner, "Sarah M. Grimké's 'Sisters of Charity,' *SIGNS*, vol. I, no. 1 (Autumn 1975), 246–56, and Gerda Lerner, "Comment on Lerner's 'Sarah M. Grimké's "Sisters of Charity," ' " *SIGNS*, vol. X, no. 4 (Summer 1985), 811–815; Sarah M. Grimké, "Marriage," in Gerda Lerner, *The Female Experience: An American Documentary* (Indianapolis: Bobbs-Merrill, 1977), 87–98.

2. Gerda Lerner, *The Creation of Feminist Consciousness: From the Middle Ages to Eighteen-Seventy* (New York: Oxford University Press, 1993), chap. 7.

3. Elizabeth Ann Bartlett (ed.), *Sarah Grimké, Letters on the Equality of the Sexes and Other Essays* (New Haven: Yale University Press, 1988), 6.

4. Angelina Emily Grimké, *Letters to Catherine E. Beecher, in Reply to an Essay on Slavery and Abolitionism, Addressed to A. E. Grimké* (Boston: Isaac Knapp, 1838); Sarah Moore Grimké, *Letters on the Equality of the Sexes and the Condition of Woman* (Boston: Isaac Knapp, 1838).

5. Letter, Sarah Grimké to Harriot Hunt, Dec. 31, 1852. Theodore Dwight Weld Collection, William L. Clements Library, University of Michigan, Ann Arbor. Hereafter referred to as WELD MSS.

6. Sarah Grimké, Diary, WELD MSS.

7. Catherine H. Birney, *Sarah and Angelina Grimké: The First American Women Advocates of Abolition and Woman's Rights* (Boston: Lee & Shepard, 1885), 28. For a detailed description of the impact of her father's death on Sarah see Lerner, Grimké biography, chap. 4.

8. Birney, *Sarah and Angelina Grimké*, 28–33. Quotes, 31, 33.

9. Sarah M. Grimké, Diary, dated 9th Month 1830, WELD MSS.

10. Sarah Grimké, Diary, entries 1827 to 1831, WELD MSS.

11. This presents problems to the historian in assigning authorship of particular works to one or the other sister, although in some cases authorship is clearly identified. I will deal with this case by case.

12. Angelina Emily Grimké, *Slavery and the Boston Riot: A Letter to Wm. L. Garrison* (Philadelphia: August 30, 1835). Broadside.

13. Sarah Grimké to Theodore Weld, [about March 10, 1837], WELD MSS. Reprinted in Gilbert H. Barnes and Dwight L. Dumond (eds.), *Letters of Theodore Dwight Weld, Angelina Grimké Weld and Sarah Grimké: 1822–1844*, 2 vols. (Gloucester, Mass: Peter Smith, 1965), I: 373. Hereafter referred to as LET.

14. Angelina Emily Grimké, *An Appeal to the Christian Women of the Southern States* (New York: n.n., 1836).

15. Sarah Moore Grimké, *An Epistle to the Clergy of the Southern States* (New York: n.n., 1836); Theodore Dwight Weld, *The Bible Against Slavery* (New York: American Anti-Slavery Society, 1837).

16. Sarah Grimké had early understood the significance for the antislavery cause of the 1832 debate on slavery in the Virginia House of Delegates. In a letter to Theodore Weld, Dec. 9, 1836, she offered to copy, edit and annotate the debate for publication by the AASS. Apparently, her offer was not taken up. See LET I:348–49.

17. William Lloyd Garrison, *Address Delivered before the Free People of Color* (Boston: S. Foster, 1831); Lydia Maria Child, *Brief History of the Condition of Women in Various Ages and Nations* (Boston: John Allen & Co., 1835).

18. Teaching offer to Angelina, see Letter, Mary and Asa Mahan to Weld, Feb. 21, 1836 [1837], WELD MSS, reprinted in LET I:360–61; for offer to Sarah see Letter, Sarah and Angelina Grimké to Weld, May 18, 1837, WELD MSS.

19. Sarah M. Grimké to Anne Warren Weston, NY 4th Mo 7th 1837, WELD MSS, reprinted in LET I:128.

20. For a fuller discussion of the sisters' contribution to the struggle against

race prejudice see Gerda Lerner, "The Grimké Sisters and the Struggle against Race Prejudice," *Journal of Negro History,* vol. XLVIII, no. 4 (Oct. 1963); Doc. 18 this volume.

21. Their leading role in the Convention is evident in the frequency with which they are cited in the record. Out of 34 substantive (non-procedural) resolutions moved and passed at the convention, Sarah offered four and Angelina eleven.

22. All citations from the convention are from Proceedings, *Anti-Slavery Convention of American Women, Held by Adjournment from the 9th to the 12th May, 1837* (New York: W. S. Dorr, 1837).

23. Angelina Emily Grimké, *An Appeal to the Women of the Nominally Free States; Issued by an Anti-Slavery Convention of American Women & Held by Adjournment from the 9th to the 12th of May, 1837.* 1st ed. (New York: W. S. Dorr, 1837); Sarah Moore Grimké, *Address to Free Colored Americans.* No printed copy is available, but the pamphlet was listed as being prepared for publication by the above convention at the same time as Angelina's pamphlet.

24. Theodore Dwight Weld to Sarah and Angelina Grimké, New York, August 26, 1837, LET I:432–36, quote, 436.

25. First quote: Angelina Grimké to Weld and John Greenleaf Whittier, Brookline [Mass.] 8th mo. 20—[1837], LET I:427–32, 428; second quote: Sarah and Angelina Grimké to Henry C. Wright, Brookline [Mass.] 8/27/37, *Ibid.,* 436–41, 437, 438.

26. Angelina Grimké, *Letters to Beecher,* Citation, Letter XII, 120–21.

27. Margaret Fuller, *Woman in the Nineteenth Century* (1845) (New York: Norton, 1971).

28. Sarah had read the following and cited them in her letters and writings: Adam Clarke, *The Epistle of Paul, the Apostle to the Romans* (Cincinnati: Jos. Mitchel, 1821); Adam Clarke, *A New Concordance to the Holy Scriptures in a Single Alphabet,* John Butterworth (ed.) (Philadelphia: J. B. Lippincott, 1846); Jonathan Dymond, *Essays on the Principles of Morality* (New York: Collins, 1844); William Paley, *Treatise on Moral and Political Philosophy* (Boston: John West, 1810); Robert Mackenzie Beverly, . . . *The Present State of the Visible Church of Christ* (London: Simpkin, Marshell & Co., 1839).

29. Margaret Fell, *Woman's Speaking Justified, Proved and Allowed by the Scriptures* . . . , (1667). The Augustan Reprint Society, No. 194 (Los Angeles: Wm. Andrews Clark Memorial Library, University of California, 1979).

30. *Equality.* First quote, 4; second, 16.

31. Luther's statement reads: *"Gott helfe mir. Hier stehe ich; ich kann nicht anders."* (God help me. Here I stand. I cannot do otherwise.)

32. *Equality*, 4, 5.
33. Quotes, *Ibid.*, 7. Mary Astell had earlier used the "prophecy" argument, as well as arguing that there was patriarchal bias in the Bible translations. But, again, Sarah Grimké had no knowledge of Astell's work.

    It is significant that in a recent excellent treatment of the story of Eve by the biblical archeologist Carol Meyers, *Discovering Eve* (Chapel Hill: University of North Carolina Press, 1994), the translation argument and Grimké's interpretation of the passage as prophecy are used without any reference to Grimké's prior work. Even in 1994 women do not know the work of women preceding their own.
34. *Equality*, 11.
35. C.f. Jean Fagan Yellin, *Women and Sisters: The Antislavery Feminists in American Culture* (New Haven: Yale University Press, 1989); Jean Fagan Yellin and John C. Van Horne (eds.), *The Abolitionist Sisterhood: Women's Political Culture in Antebellum America* (Ithaca: Cornell University Press, 1994).
36. *Equality*, 19.
37. *Ibid.*, 60.
38. *Ibid.*, 22, 23.
39. *Ibid.*, 118.
40. Lydia Maria Child, *Brief History of the Condition of Women in Various Ages and Nations* (Boston: John Allen & Co., 1835), 2 vols.
41. For example, she charges the Apostle Paul's misogynist statements to the fact that "his mind was under the influence of Jewish prejudices respecting women" and quotes Clarke as her source. *Equality*, 91 and 111–12. The reference is probably to Adam Clarke, *Commentary on the Holy Scriptures*. Elsewhere in the text she refers to the "Jewish nation" as guilty of crucifying Christ, 68.
42. Quote on political rights, *Equality*, 74; quote on free agents, 121–22; indented quote, 122–23. Emphasis and capitalization by Grimké.
43. See Bartlett for a discussion of the work's history. See also Lucy Stone to Francis Stone, Aug. 31, 1838, Blackwell Family Papers, Library of Congress, as cited in Blanche Glassman Hersh, *The Slavery of Sex: Feminist-Abolitionists in America* (Urbana: University of Illinois Press, 1978), 85. Lucretia Mott quote: Otelia Cromwell, *Lucretia Mott*, (Cambridge: Harvard University Press, 1958), 145.
44. The work is available in a Source Book Press reprint and is included in Bartlett.
45. [Theodore Dwight Weld], *American Slavery As It Is: Testimony of a Thousand Witnesses* (New York: American Anti-Slavery Society, 1839).

46. *Ibid.*, 22–23.
47. Angelina Grimké Weld to Mary Grimké, ca. 1853, WELD MSS. I date this letter Spring 1852.
48. Sarah Grimké to Harriot Hunt, Dec. 31, 1852, WELD MSS.
49. Katherine Du Pre Lumpkin in her biography, *The Emancipation of Angelina Grimké* (Chapel Hill: University of North Carolina Press, 1974) depicts Sarah as the evil force in Angelina's life and blames the crisis entirely on her. She goes so far as to state that Angelina's "relationship with Sarah had brought disaster" [to Angelina] (p. 201). I strongly disagree with this interpretation, which disregards the social circumstances of both sisters' lives, and treats Sarah Grimké as historically insignificant except as a negative influence in her sister's life.
50. Sarah Grimké to Harriot Hunt, Dec. 31, 1852, WELD MSS.
51. For a fuller treatment of the subject, see Ann Braude, *Radical Spirits: Spiritualism and Women's Rights in Nineteenth-Century America* (Boston: Beacon Press, 1989). Among the many prominent reformers who believed in Spiritualism and participated in Spiritualist seances were William Lloyd Garrison, Joshua Giddings, Robert Dale Owen Jr., Lydia Maria Child, Frances Dana Gage, and Mary Todd Lincoln, the President's wife.
52. Sarah M. Grimké, "The Education of Women," in Bartlett, 116. Citations within text will hereafter be referenced to this printed source.
53. *Ibid.* First paragraph, 116. Next paragraph, 117.
54. Sarah Grimké, "Marriage," MSS in WELD MSS. Unnumbered pp. As reprinted in Gerda Lerner, *The Female Experience: An American Documentary* (New York: Oxford University Press, 1992). All page references are to this printed edition.

    The authenticity of this essay, which I have assigned to Sarah Grimké, has been challenged by Professor Carl Degler on the grounds that the manuscript is in Angelina's handwriting.

    The handwriting evidence does not seem decisive to me. The sisters often copied each other's letters, speeches and articles. I did a thorough study of this essay, comparing it with other work of Sarah's, and find in the manuscript many parallels, even whole phrases, used earlier by Sarah. Many of the ideas and concerns expressed in this essay appear in her correspondence and other writings. I will try here to show some of these parallels but will not attempt to include all of them. See Doc. 11.
55. Grimké, "Marriage," 95–96. The same idea is expressed in her essay "Education of Women," cited above, 32.
56. Grimké, "Marriage," 96.
57. Letter, Sarah Grimké to Harriot Hunt, June 28, 1857, WELD MSS, Box 11.

58. The reference to the Crimean War makes it possible to date these notes as having been written in 1856 or shortly thereafter. Sarah Grimké, "Essay on the Laws Respecting Women," WELD MSS, reprinted in Bartlett. All page reference are to this printed version. Quote, 136.

59. Sarah Grimké, "Lecture Notes," written on Eagleswood School Announcement, dated April 18, 1856. Quote, Lecture 14.

60. The full title is Mrs. Anna Jameson, *Sisters of Charity and the Communion of Labour: Two Lectures on the Social Employment of Women*, 2d rev. ed. (London: Longmans, Brown and Green, 1855). For details on my discovery of the origins of this essay twenty years after I completed my biography of the Grimké Sisters, see Gerda Lerner, "Comment on Lerner's 'Sarah M. Grimké's "Sisters of Charity," ' " *SIGNS: Journal of Women in Culture and Society*, vol. 10, no. 4 (Summer 1985), 811–15. Sarah Grimké's Essay "Sisters of Charity" was reprinted in Gerda Lerner, "Sarah M. Grimké's 'Sisters of Charity,' "*SIGNS*, vol. 1, no.1 (Autumn, 1975), 246–56. Quotes from this essay in the text will be referenced to the page numbers in this *SIGNS* reprint.

61. "Sisters of Charity," *SIGNS*, 252.

62. Quotes, *ibid.*, 252, 253, 254.

63. Sarah M. Grimké "The Education of Women," WELD MSS. Published in Bartlett, 104–25. Quote from Bartlett, 124.

64. The stereotyped notion that the antislavery reformers were all middle class needs correction. The Grimké sisters, Lydia Maria Child, Harriet Hanson Robinson, Jane Elizabeth Jones, Abby Kelley and Stephen Foster, to name a few, lived spartan lives on a poverty income level. One should investigate not their origins but their chosen life styles to arrive at a more accurate understanding of their economic situation.

65. "Sisters of Charity," 162–63.

66. Ellen DuBois, "On Labor and Free Love: Two Unpublished Speeches of Elizabeth Cady Stanton," *SIGNS*, vol. I, no. 1 (Autumn 1975), 257–68, esp. 265–68.

67. Letter, Sarah M. Grimké to Sarah Wattles, March 24, 1856, Weld MSS, Box 11.

68. *Ibid.*

69. Sarah Grimké to Sarah Wattles, June 1, 1856, WELD MSS.

70. Sarah Grimké to ?, undated, WELD MSS.

71. Letter, Sarah M. Grimké to Katherine Brooks Yale, Feb. 9, 1870, WELD MSS, Box 13.

DOCUMENTS

❧ 1 ❧

Letter to Queen Victoria

The sisters wrote this letter during their New England speaking tour. It is not clear whether they ever mailed it. They may have intended to send it to a British reform journal so as to make their appeal to a wider audience.

What is remarkable about the letter is the feminist assumption that they can and should address the Queen as a sister and appeal to her in the name of their common womanhood. The self-confident, even somewhat arrogant tone of their appeal expresses their sense of moral superiority as spokespersons for the oppressed. ("We do not apologize for writing this letter . . .") Their familiarity with the issues of West Indian Emancipation and with the activities of British abolitionists is also worth noting. It derived from their association with the British abolitionist George Thompson, who had toured New England together with Garrison; with the British antislavery and temperance lecturer Charles Stuart, a close friend of Theodore Weld, who had been mobbed in western New York in 1835 while on a lecture tour; and from their correspondence with the British Quaker and reformer Elisabeth Pease and with several British female antislavery societies.

❧❧❧❧

Sarah and Angelina Grimké to Queen Victoria. Garrison Papers and Weston Papers, both Boston Public Library.*

Addressed: Victoria Queen of Great Britain

Boston, October 26, 1837

Dear Sister

Accustomed as thou art to receive the homage of an admiring nation, we know not how thou wilt be prepared to receive a communication from two women who dare not approach thee with the language of adulation. We feel that as moral and immortal beings we all stand on the same platform of *Human Rights* and therefore that we have the same duties and the same responsibilities. But altho' as women, we are in common with thyself invested with privileges and bound by obligations, yet we are sensible, that as Queen of a mighty people, thou hast peculiar duties and great responsibilities; and we earnestly desire for thee that child-like dependence on the Lord Jesus Christ which will enable thee to perform thy duties as unto God and not unto man. We rejoice that as far as we have been able to understand thy character, thou art qualified by education to fill the throne of England; but dear Sister, we entreat thee to seek that wisdom which cometh from above, which is first pure, then peaceable gentle and easy to be entreated, full of mercy and good fruits. So shall a crown of glory encircle thy brow far exceeding the splendor of diamonds and rubies.

We will briefly mention that our birth place is Charleston South Carolina, one of the slave states of this American Union, that we were reared in the midst of the system of slavery, and can testify from personal observation and knowledge to the horrors and abominations which are inseparable from it. Our hearts have long been deeply moved by the sufferings of the unhappy slaves in this country, we are self-exiled from the hearth stone of our fathers, because we could not endure the sight of that misery we were powerless to relieve. Within a few years we have been cheered by the rise of Anti Slavery Societies and a hope has dawned that the day of deliverance for the desolate captives in our land already draweth nigh. Animated

* Reprinted by permission, courtesy of the Trustees of the Boston Public Library.

with this hope, we have been going from city to city and village to village during the past year, holding public meetings with our brethren and sisters and pleading the cause of outraged humanity. In the prosecution of this work we have been strengthened and encouraged by hearing that thou hadst prorogued [discontinued a session of] Parliament *in person*, because our public addresses have been denounced by many as inconsistent with the modesty of woman and with the duties of that sphere, which it is said *God has ordained* that woman shall move in, but which in reality has been assigned her by man.

We have watched with intense solicitude the progress of the cause of liberty in thy dominions; the names of British Philanthropists are dear to our hearts; and we rejoiced when we heard that King William had set his seal to the liberation of the West India slaves. We have been grieved tho' not disappointed, at the failure of the scheme of apprenticeship, and are thankful that it has been exhibited in such striking contrast with the happy effects of Immediate Emancipation in the islands of Antigua and Bermuda. We know the heart of the slave holder so well, that it requires no prophets eye for us to foresee, that he would abuse all the power left in his hands, and treat his victims with added cruelty, because in a little while they were to be rescued from his grasp.

We write now to entreat thee on behalf of the down trodden millions in our own country, and the hundreds of thousands in thy dominions to abolish the system of apprenticeship which is fraught with so much suffering to the slaves, to open thine ear to the cry of the oppressed and rid them out of the hand of the oppressor. As Americans, much more as Christians, we feel deeply interested in this cause. The moral power of England will be felt in every part of our beloved country, aiding and animating those who are laboring for the overthrow of slavery. We are grateful for the thrilling appeals which thy countrymen and countrywomen have sent to the United States, they have been spirit stirring and have strengthened the hands and comforted the hearts of abolitionists.

America is awfully guilty; she has professed herself a Republic, whilst cherishing in her bosom a confederacy of petty tyrants, who are not exceeded in power, nor surpassed in cruelty, by any despots whose blood stained annals disgrace the page of history. She has assumed to be the freest nation in the world, whilst hundreds of thousands of her native born children are wearing the chains of hopeless bondage. She has arrogated to herself the title of the most enlightened nation in the world, while her code of slave laws is written in blood, and she justifies her impious attempt to *annihilate the mind* of a portion of her citizens by the tyrants plea—Necessity—. America boasts of having declared the African slave trade piracy, yet her Congress permits and sanctions the interstate slavetrade. This traffic in the persons of men amounted last year to 200,000 and is replete with nearly equal misery to those wretched beings who are torn from their homes and their families to suit the convenience, or gratify the avarice, of their owners. She professes to be a Christian nation, whilst her ministry and her church thro'out the land, with some honorable exceptions are sustaining the bloodstained temple of the Moloch of slavery.

We are persuaded that this nation must be overwhelmed in ruin except we repent. Already do we hear the distant mutterings of the exterminating thunder of Gods retributive justice. We appeal unto thee O Queen! and beseech thee by the mercies of God, to undo the heavy burdens in thy dominions and break every yoke; that we in America, seeing thy good work may glorify God, and be stimulated to do likewise. We also entreat thee to consider the case of our poor suffering brethren and sisters in Canada. There is not a foot of ground in all the republican despotism of America, where they are safe from their merciless oppressors. When they flee from the task masters of the South, they are compelled to traverse the whole length of the *nominally* free states to find a city of refuge on British soil. O let them find it there indeed! Knowest thou not that even there the slaveholder has pursued the unhappy fugitive, and seized his victim under pretext of having committed some crime? God grant that these hunted and stricken ones may have thy sympathy, and that thou mayest obey the command "Let mine outcasts dwell with thee, be thou a covert to them from the force of the spoiler."

Our hearts have been gladdened by the information, that the women of Great Britain are preparing a petition to be presented to thee, relative to the Apprenticeship system. May the Lord incline thine ear to hear, and thy heart to grant their prayer. A *Queen* first legalized the African slave trade in England, and it is our fervent desire that a *Queen* may burst the bonds of every slave over whom her sovereignty extends, that the blessing of those who are ready to perish may come upon Victoria, and her memory be embalmed in the hearts of Christians, wherever her name is known. Is not the subject of slavery worthy of thy attention. Is it not one of the greatest that can engage the mind of man. Is not its extinction intimately connected with the advancement of Christ's kingdom?

Sister we do not apologize for writing this letter, it is the offspring of love to thy soul, of love to the enslaved every where. Receive it in love from those, who have no claim to thy notice, save that they are pleading for God's outraged poor.

We are thine in those bonds of humanity and Christianity which bind together the nations of the earth in a common brotherhood.

SARAH M GRIMKÉ
ANGELINA E GRIMKÉ

❧ 2 ❧

SMG to Augustus Wattles

The following letter, one of several written to her friends, describes Sarah's unhappy state of mind in 1852. Her wish to have money, so as to be able to help those she most loved, is a response to the straitened circumstances in which the Weld/Grimké family found itself after several years of running a boarding school at their Belleville, N. J., farm. Angelina had suffered from debilitating ill health, and both Sarah and Weld had had bouts of pneumonia and fever. The school was not paying their expenses and the family would within a few months make a major move to the newly-formed utopian cooperative settlement of Raritan Bay Union.

At the time of the writing of this letter the future of the family was uncertain, and Sarah was already contemplating a separation from the family. The reference to "Theodore's children" is telling and occurs several times during her correspondence in these years. Sometimes she simply refers to them as "the children," but seldom as "Angelina's children." The conflict with Angelina over her role as surrogate mother of her sister's children was already brewing, even though it had been suppressed by both sisters. A few months later, Angelina would openly state her hurt feelings to Sarah and encourage her to leave the family and live on her own. Sarah, who dreaded the idea of living in a commune and felt hurt by Angelina's complaints, actually did move away and tried to think of ways of making a living on her own. Her review, in this letter, of her flawed education reflects her thinking about starting a career so late in her life.

৯ৡৡ

February 15 1852

. . . Oh Augustus I do sometimes desire wealth just that I might place in comfort and independence those in whom I am so much interested. But this like all my other earthly phantoms of happiness has never been fulfilled and at 60 I look back on a life of deep disappointment of withered hopes, of unlooked for suffering of severe discipline. Yet I have sometimes tasted exquisite joys and have found a solace for many a woe in the innocence and earnest love of Theodore's children. But for this my life would have little to record of mundane pleasures. In early youth I was a worldling but I enjoyed not its frivolities; there was a sting in them which poisoned them. I was naturally independent, longed for an education that would elevate me above the low pursuits of sense, but I was a girl and altho' well educated as such, yet the powers of my mind were not called into exercise. I looked with longing eyes on my brother's superior advantages and wondered why the simple fact of being a girl should shut me up to the necessity of being a doll a coquette, a fashionable fool—my haughty spirit spurned the idea of being dependent on my father and strange and curious and various were the fancies that crowded my juvenile years to attain education and independence, but I thought to no purpose save to render me more dissatisfied and all my vain imaginings came to naught. Next came the religious era. But it is past, the phantoms of pleasure and pain have perished. I am still a "would be something higher, better." . . .

❧ 3 ❧

SMG to the Editors of the
Christian Inquirer

In the following three "Letters to the Editor" (Docs. 3, 4, 5) Sarah Grimké develops ideas which will find more complete expression in the three essay fragments below. There are references in many of her letters during 1852 and 1853 to her intention to write another book on women and to her working on several "essays." The topic was of growing interest in reform circles, no doubt due to the annual woman's rights conventions, which assembled in various parts of the Northeast. In the text below Sarah refers specifically to the convention held at Worcester, Massachusetts, in 1851.

In this document she responds to an editorial written in the *New York Christian Inquirer,* a Unitarian newspaper, by its editor, the Rev. Henry Bellows, after that convention. The Rev. Bellows reported on this second Worcester convention with enthusiasm: ". . . [I]t seems to us to be the most important meeting since that held in the cabin of the *Mayflower,"* and topped this endorsement by stating that this reform [woman's rights] surpasses in significance "any other now . . . if it do not outweigh Magna Charta [*sic*] and our Declaration themselves."* The Rev. Bellows confessed himself to be among those who

* All quotations are from Rev. Henry Bellows, D. D., "The Woman's Rights Convention at Worcester," in Elizabeth Cady Stanton, Susan B. An-

had regarded the first Worcester woman's rights convention (1850) with "distrust and distate." Despite his conversion and new-found enthusiasm for the cause, he used most of his editorial to caution women not to be bitter and judgmental in their attitude towards men. "If the female sex is injured in its present position, it is an injury growing out of . . . an honest error, in which the sexes have conspired." He defended the construction of "separate spheres" as natural, based on "superior bodily strength on the masculine side, and of maternity on the feminine side." He concluded that women should regard the opposition they will encounter as "founded on prejudices that are not selfish, but merely masculine."

Sarah ignored his patronizing assumption that women needed his instruction on how to conduct the struggle for their emancipation, but she used forceful language in rebuttal. Women, she wrote, feel that they are "forcibly restrained in the exercise of their rights," that they are "hemmed in on every side . . . , perishing for lack of intellectual culture, . . . starving for want of food to sustain mere animal existence, . . . restive, they look round to find their oppressors."* She considered it natural that women, so long wronged, should be "belligerent . . . and that they determine to contend for their rights." This passage echoes the militancy of her earliest feminist statement: "All I ask of our brethren is, that they will take their feet off our necks, and permit us to stand upright on that ground which God designed us to occupy."**

She continued in her letter to trace a history of the relations of the sexes, a theme which will recur in most of the writings of her later years. Her explanation in this letter does not reach very far, and Sarah abandons it in order to touch upon a subject that preoccupied her at the time and one that we will see her elaborate more fully in the essay—the evils for women of marriage based solely on their need for economic support. She ends her letter with a fervent plea for the independence of women.

---

thony and Matilda Joselyn Gage (eds.), *History of Woman Suffrage: 1848–1861*, 2 vols. (New York:Fowler and Wells, 1881), 1:243–44.

 * Quotations from document printed below.

 ** Sarah Moore Grimké, *Letters on the Equality of the Sexes and the Condition of Woman* (Boston: Isaac Knapp, 1838), 10.

ᏩᎧᏩᎧᏩᎧ

Belleville, [New Jersey,] February 10, 1852

To the Editors of the Christian Inquirer:

I thank you most cordially in the name of my sex, in the name of humanity, for the sentiments expressed in your article on the Worcester Convention. Greatly do many who are engaged in that reform need to have such views thrown before them. They feel in their utmost being that their rights are coequal with those of their brethren; that they are forcibly restrained in the exercise of their rights; that the place allotted them is too narrow for their growth to that stature to which God designs them to attain. Hemmed in on every side, perishing for lack of intellectual culture themselves, and seeing thousands around them starving for want of food to sustain mere animal existence, they grow restive; they look round to find their oppressors and see that those whom they have been taught to regard as protectors, whose admiration they have sought, whose praise and flattery they have won, are in possession of the fair fields of science and literature, of all the most lucrative professions and trades; that woman's labor, though equally well or better performed is deemed unworthy the same remuneration. They do not pause to inquire how these things have come to pass; they feel the present pressure, and, taking counsel of impatience and suffering, place themselves in a belligerent attitude, and determine to contend for their rights. This is natural; the inevitable consequence of feeling the privation of rights. But it is time to take a more enlarged, and generous, and philosophical view of this whole subject, to cease the tirade about tyranny, oppression, and wilful [sic] injustice, and soberly ask ourselves how woman came to occupy her present relative position?

In the infancy of the human race, the physical part of our being was first unfolded. Strength and prowess were the chief glory of man; hence the stronger exercised dominion over the weaker, not over the weaker *sex* only, but over all of their own sex whom they could bring into subjection. This was the natural result of the then undeveloped state of mankind. Just in proportion as man has progressed, he has lifted his foot from the neck of his victims; and just as soon as woman is prepared to fulfil the glorious destiny which awaits her, as the equal, companion, and co-laborer of man, she will find the path open before her, and none to forbid her entrance. Men are not unwilling to see woman elevated; their scruples respecting her assuming a new position in society are honest in the mass, and so soon as they see that the progress and development of the human race are intimately linked with independence of thought, word, and deed, in woman, they will help her to fulfil her high vocation. I am mistaken if the pioneers in this reform do not find their sturdiest opponents in their own ranks, and almost necessarily so. As a body, women have not had the means of being as highly developed intellectually as men. They have not been accustomed to take enlarged and comprehensive views, to think for themselves, to reason out a point and form their own conclusions; but, adhering to the advice of the apostle, (which doubtless was called for in his day,) they have been contented to ask their husbands', brothers', or sons' counsel, and to base their opinions upon what they might say. Hence, when such a question comes to be mooted as the equal rights of the sexes, men will be likely sooner to see its justice and the results which will follow; and I greatly overrate my brethren if they are not willing to yield to us what humanity, equity, and the good of the race imperatively call for in our day—equal rights, and equal means of development and usefulness.

Man cannot fail to see that the elevation of woman must react upon himself; that as they are *one* by the immutable laws of God, everything that produces a higher tone of character in her, that makes her an independent, thinking being, will be so much capital in his hands to improve his own intellectual and spiritual nature. He cannot fail to see that if woman has opened to her all the means of independence, of self-support, of accumulating property, that it will relieve him of an immense burden, often too heavy to bear, as the wrinkled brow and care-worn furrows testify. In what is called genteel society, multitudes of women are a dead weight upon their fathers, husbands, or brothers. I do not blame, I pity them. Education has rendered them helpless, and they drag out an existence even more miserable than belongs to those whom they oppress; the prey of ennui, because they have no object in life, no end to accomplish, no duties to fulfil [*sic*]. If they are young, they have a reasonable expectation that they may marry, and by this means insure a permanent living. Thousands are thus sacrificed, either by their parents

or themselves, who, had they been educated in honorable independence, and been able to earn a livelihood by their own exertions,
would have scorned so to violate the sacredness of those feelings
which God has given as a safeguard to domestic happiness. Too
much importance cannot be attached to the independence of
woman. Her present dependent condition is fraught with every evil,
for to act consciously, uprightly, unswervingly true to God and ourselves, while dependent for daily bread upon those who differ from
us in opinion, and use all their influence to induce us to surrender
our judgment to theirs, is one of the highest and rarest of human
achievements.

Hoping that the subject may claim your further attention, and
that the public will hear from you again, I remain respectfully,

SARAH M. GRIMKÉ

⚘ 4 ⚘

SMG to the Editor of
The Lily

In this brief essay Sarah Grimké argues more strongly than she has previously that women must stop asking men for favors. They must "strike for freedom" and *assert* their rights. This stance may reflect the increased self-confidence of feminists following upon the successful woman's rights conventions at Seneca Falls, N.Y., 1848; Salem, Ohio, 1850; Worcester, Mass., 1851; and Syracuse, N.Y., 1852. Sarah took a keen interest in these conventions and read the proceedings in the reform papers. She also corresponded with participants and urged her friends to attend the conventions. The effect of the conventions on participants and sympathizers was to convince them of the need for collective public action in behalf of woman, and Sarah here reflects that new consciousness.

As she had done earlier in her work, Sarah cast the movement for woman's rights in the mold of the American Revolution. In effect, she characterized it as the unfinished task of the American Revolution. This coming revolution would not free half of the human race only, thus it would be more glorious than the Revolution of '76.

In line with this Lockean argument, Grimké specifies the various professions to which woman should lay claim. Significantly she includes the right to be a juror. This was an advanced argument for her time.

The quote from Horace Mann is from one of his lectures printed in the *Daily Tribune,* to which Sarah would respond shortly after in the form of an open letter (see Doc. 5).

ঔঌঔঌঔঌ

Sarah M. Grimké to *The Lily,* April 1852, p. 27.

IF YOU WOULD HAVE FREEDOM, STRIKE FOR IT

"They are unworthy of freedom who do not strike for it," said Washington. This truth was burned into the souls of the men and women of the Revolution, and braced their arms and nerved their hearts in the day of peril and of suffering. They did well in their generation and achieved for themselves and for the world, the greatest victory that had yet been achieved, a victory over the despotism of sovereigns on the one hand, and over the popular opinion of the world on the other, by establishing a Republic based upon the great principles of liberty and equality, for half the human race. Is it too much to say that a greater Revolution is now pending? Shall I adopt the language of the Father of our country, and in view of this Revolution, say to the women of America, "They are unworthy of freedom who do not strike for it."! Nay, my sisters, but I do say we are unworthy of freedom, if we do not labor and suffer for its attainment. . . . The revolution I now plead for is a revolution that will not bless one half of the human family only. It will spread its panoply of love over all mankind, and secure to woman also, those inalienable rights, which are the gift of God, and when enjoyed by ALL, will work out for ALL a far more exceeding weight of glory than the Revolution of '76.

Too many of those who are engaged in the present reform, seem to suppose that the great work we have to do is to look to our fathers and brothers for help, and accept it when they grant it. True, we need their aid. To work efficiently and harmoniously, we must work together; but on woman rests the responsibility of elevating woman. The time has passed by when her most effective weapons were tears, and sighs and bended knees. To these, man has rarely been insensible. The helpless babe has never stretched its arms to him for protection, but it has found a nestling place in man's great heart. To him has woman seldom raised the supplicating eye in vain. . . .

As long as woman used such means to gain her end, she proclaimed her inability to help herself, her need of the strong arm and the brave heart of man to shelter and protect her. Incapable of framing laws for her own government it naturally and necessarily devolved on those whose intellect was more developed, and whose physical powers had placed them in the position of superiors. But in the progress of the race, woman begins to feel, that although she always has been, and probably always will be inferior to man in physical endowments, yet that she has moral and intellectual gifts now sufficiently developed to qualify her for a loftier position in society. She feels that instead of approaching man with sighs, and tears, and supplications, she must do it by reasoning, by argument, by the force of moral truth, that he, as well as she, has progressed, and that his intellectual and spiritual nature will appreciate the truths she utters, as easily as his sensuous nature formerly understood her sorrows and her entreaties. She feels that physical force . . . [should] no longer control the destiny of man; that those qualities with which she has been endowed as a moral and intellectual being, are the qualities which are now needed to help her brethren to fulfil [sic] their mission. We have long enough stood idle. Horace Mann says, "a man must marry a dozen women, to get one worthy of the name of wife." Well, be it so; I have no disposition to break a lance about our deficiencies. Let us rather concentrate our energies to remedy them, and to make ourselves what we are designed to be—co-laborers in the development of the race.

The law of progress is proclaimed by every page of human history, and whether we aid or retard the work, it still goes on, and they only are losers who oppose its progress. Let woman appeal to Legislative and Ecclesiastical bodies, as well as to Medical Colleges, setting forth the injury inflicted on humanity by the present laws and rules. Let her go herself before those public bodies, and set forth the difficulties under which she labors, the disabilities which are imposed upon her, the injustice of taxation without representation, and of not permitting her to be tried by a jury of her peers. It is objected to this last innovation, that if women sat as jurors, the sentences on woman would be less lenient than they now are. I shall not dispute this; time only can settle it. But admitting that it is so— that the sexes are more merciful to each other than to themselves, then so much greater the reason for woman to share the toil and the responsibility of jurorship. Let there be an interchange of good offices, that men may experience from them the mercy they have failed to find in man. Woman has a deep, intuitive, divine sense of justice, and she has a power of endurance, of quiet fortitude in bearing fatigue, hunger, thirst, and sleeplessness, at least equal to man. Or if she has not, a superior education, by giving her habits of close attention and continued concentration of mind, will qualify her for the responsibility of jurorship. Of this I am very certain, if woman is not capable of fulfilling the duties of that post, she will not be elevated to it, or, if elevated, will soon vacate it. Character and ability, like water, will find their level as a general fact; and this accounts for the present position of woman. She is just beginning to realize her wealth of mind, and moral power.

SARAH M. GRIMKÉ

❦ 5 ❦

SMG to the Editors,
New York Daily Tribune

In April 1852, Horace Mann (1796–1859), the educator and Massachusetts state legislator, gave two lectures at the Tabernacle on the subject "A Word to a Young Woman." He opened his condemnation of "a new theory of equality of the sexes" with a sarcastic reference to a woman he termed "the leader of this sect in Europe," Helen Maria Weber of Hamburg who dresses and behaves like a man, and claims equality with the sterner sex."* Having thus identified American woman's rights advocates with cross-dressers—a favorite mode of attack from that time to this—he proceeded to develop a traditional defense of separate spheres for the two sexes. He deplored the absence of women from history which he concluded was due to their having made no worthwhile contributions to it; threw in a gratuitous antisemitic remark; condemned women's economic exploitation and deplored her inadequate education. In his second lecture he developed his attack on the inadequate education of women and urged improvement. Then followed a lengthy elaboration of traditional gender stereotypes: women were fitted best for housekeeping, childcare, decorating and the "more quiet and retired professions and trades."

* All citations in this headnote are from Hon. Horace Mann, "A Word to a Young Woman," *New York Daily Tribune*, Feb. 23, 1852, 6 and *ibid.*, April 19, 1852, 7.

His one concession to contemporary trends was to strongly endorse women's education and urge opportunities for women in medicine and nursing. But women, according to Horace Mann, were utterly unsuited for law, jury duty, and the dirty world of politics. If women wanted glory, let them be directed toward work in philanthropy and moral improvement.

This, from the outstanding educator of the ante-bellum period. Sarah Grimké's answer, addressed to Horace Mann, is quite mild in tone and takes up only one of his points, namely that "woman has been little more than the mother of the race." Grimké argues that woman developed together with man, although functioning in a different sphere, and that her contributions to civilization have not been properly acknowledged. She takes the argument further by urging men to be actively involved in the home as fathers and she even hints that the institutions of society should be changed to allow for this to happen. Unfortunately, her flowery style in the last two sentences of this excerpt somewhat obscures her radical meaning.

§↰§↰§↰

To the Editors of the N.Y. Tribune:*

The following thoughts have been elicited by the lectures of Horace Mann on Woman, as they are reported in *The Tribune*. I ask a place for them in the same paper, not because I wish to defend or excuse woman, but because these lectures contain fundamental errors, which, under the sanction of a justly esteemed name, may be received as truths.

The great thought, which has simultaneously started into life in thousands of minds, that woman is not fulfilling her vocation, that she has been disenfranchised of her rights, is the idea of the age. I do not mean that it is the grandest or noblest idea of the age, but that it does not belong to individuals; it belongs to advanced minds, is the result of development, and was kindled by the living coals of the divine altar. Let there be life, said the Infinite, and myriad voices answered, Amen!

*Sarah M. Grimké, "Horace Mann on the Woman Question," *New York Daily Tribune*, May 31, 1852. Reprinted in *The Lily*, July 1852, p. 64.

Can it be that "Woman has been little more than the mother of the race." If so, well may she bow her head in dust and ashes at the footstool of man, for *he* has raised noble monuments of moral and intellectual achievements. From his creation he has been gradually improving, rising from savageism [*sic*] and cannibalism to barbarism, thence to civilization, obtaining, as the light slowly dawned upon his soul, higher views of God and humanity. Art, Science, Literature, Religion, all bear witness to the wonders *he* has wrought, and the past gives promise for the future. While man has thus progressed, while the spiritual has been gaining an ascendancy over the animal nature, has woman remained what she was at her birth? No! side by side with her beloved "hemisphere" has she progressed. And man has not willfully or maliciously impeded her progress. If he has said in some departments of improvement, "hitherto shalt thou come and no further," he has, I think, erred through ignorance, often with the sincerest desire to do good. Is there nothing in the history of woman; nothing in her devotion to the duties of home; nothing in her patient endurance of injury; nothing in the fortitude with which she has borne suffering, weakness, obloquy, reproach; nothing in her untiring love and tender vigils at the midnight couch; nothing in her secret prayers, her unuttered aspirations for a higher destiny for herself and her brethren; nothing in the intrepidity with which she has endured martyrdom; nothing in the courage with which she is even now facing a frowning world, walking with firm yet modest step through the myriads that oppose her, and uttering in a voice of prophecy, "EXCELSIOR?". . . .

Woman has so long been accustomed to delve in the kitchen, that she needs the encouragement of man, to devote less time to the lower and more to the higher wants of her household.

"Wide as the field now open to woman is, it begins at home. Make home what it should be and then extend the work to other homes."

Is this not equally true of man? Do not his children claim from him, as well as from their mother, the consecration of his best powers—a portion of his time? Is not the influence of both parents necessary to the symmetrical development of their offspring? . . . In the present arrangements of society, children are defrauded of the care and influence of their father's [*sic*] at a period when the mind is susceptible, the will plastic, and the heart running over with love. Million voices cry to the counting house, "Give up"—to the court-house and the exchange, "Keep not back"—to the pulpit, "Remember *home*, and while you are busy dressing the vineyards of others, let not the scions from your own roots perish." . . .

⚘ 6 ⚘

SMG to Augustus Wattles

In the following two letters (Docs. 6,7) to her friends Augustus Wattles and his wife Susan, Sarah Grimké deals with the most troublesome aspect of political life, the danger of civil war in Kansas. In 1838 she and Angelina had accepted the "ultra" peace principles of Henry C. Wright and William Lloyd Garrison. As former Quakers, their commitment to non-violence and pacifism was strong. But the threat of violence by slaveholders eroded these convictions. In the following letters Sarah begins to qualify her peace principles by trying to understand what might motivate Augustus to reach for arms in defense of abolitionism and of his home.

Augustus Wattles was a friend of Theodore Weld's from his days at Lane seminary. He became superintendent of a school for free Blacks in Cincinnati, then he became one of the most effective agents of the American Anti-Slavery Society. He later moved to Kansas and served as editor of the antislavery *Herald of Freedom* in Lawrence, Kansas. His wife, Susan Lowe, was one of the abolitionist women who had come to Cincinnati in the 1830s to establish and run schools for black children. The Wattleses worked closely with African-Americans in Ohio and Indiana, establishing trade schools and a sort of farm bureau for prospective black farmers.

In the April 2,1854, letter Sarah discusses her religious beliefs, which express her search for the female aspect of the Divine. She finds this in the motherly aspects of Christ's role as nurturer of the downtrodden and as divine sacrifice. In this she follows a long line of feminist revisioners of Christian theology, beginning with female mystics such as Julian of Norwich. Grimké was, of course, unaware of their existence.

Her anti-Judaism, expressed in this letter and recurring in a few other references in her correspondence, is based on the mainstream anti-Semitism of Martin Luther and others, on the standard anti-Judaism of the theologians Grimké read and on the view prevalent in her day among Christian advocates of woman's rights that Christianity had brought the highest level of civilization and with it rights for women. In this view, while more needed to be done to give women equal rights, it was due to Christianity that they could even define and assert such rights. Proponents of this "Christian feminism" such as Harriet Beecher Stowe, Phebe Hanaford and Sarah Josepha Hale, among others, cited Christ's gentle nature against the fierceness of patriarchal Jehovah and likened the situation of Jewish women to those of "heathens." Their arguments were uniformly ignorant, but they fitted in well with popular antisemitic notions and remained generally undiscussed and unchallenged to this day. Sarah Grimké went right along.

§➤§➤§➤

Eagleswood April 2 [1854]

Beloved friends

How my heart yearns over you in your present perilous and difficult position. How earnestly I crave for you the wisdom which cometh from above. It is impossible [for me] to advise, because I feel that you must pursue existing circumstances whatever conscience dictates as the most noble, self-sacrificing course. If you have the divine guidance you need fear nothing and you can always fall back upon that and say even if it is uttered in anguish of spirit Lord thou knowest mine integrity. While there are immutable laws governing the moral universe, while *right* must ever stand in the front of those laws, and *wrong* as its opposite, we must not confound right and wrong with guilt and innocence. Intention constitutes innocence, or guilt—but if my intention to produce happiness fails, and instead thereof I produce misery, the action is wrong, altho' I am not guilty because my intention was to produce happiness—the confusion of these ideas has been productive of half the disputations, wranglings, and animosities in the world, yet the distinction is as clear as sunlight, as clear as that two and two make four. If desiring, as I have no doubt you do, to promote the best interests of the people of Kansas you religiously believe that the best means is to settle it by the sword, to become yourself a bearer of the sword and with your own hand perhaps transfer a brother man to another sphere of existence—do it dear Augustus and God speed your efforts for the race. If on the other hand you feel in the depths of your spirit that you are called to endure rather than to resist, stand by the convictions come what may. It is impossible for one to decide positively what is the right course for another to pursue under given circumstances, and as you remark "Kansas produces a rapid development of the lower faculties. No government, no religion, no women to restrain—men are not only left without these usual checks to vice, but they are aggravated by privations and wrongs." Yes, my brother, accumulated incentives to revenge, to struggling to maintain the rights appertaining to every human being, rights grievously outraged and trampled upon for the purpose of establishing slavery surround and bear hard upon you. What I should do myself I dare not say. . . . God help you and yours so to act in the crisis that you may keep a conscience void of offence. The last news I heard from Kansas gave birth to a hope that you would not be molested again by the Missourians. Yet I almost despair of seeing slavery abolished in the U.S. but by a servile and civil war—although I must confess I have no history to bear me out in the idea that slaves can attain freedom by insurrection.

Greatly do I rejoice that you have been blest in basket and in store, if I can hear by next fall that you have a comfortable dwelling, and are in the enjoyment of domestic conveniences I shall truly be thankful. My heart is linked to you and yours through our precious Sarah and I hope since providence has led her to Kansas some field of usefulness wider than the duties of home may open for her. I should not fear Sarah's undertaking even a school of rough boys—she has so much self respect, modesty and sweetness, combined I hope with firmness, that I think she would secure the respect of others and subdue by gentleness, meekness and love. Great is the sway which a true woman holds over the other sex and quite lately I was reading somewhere that Experience had proved that women were better qualified morally to keep just such schools than men. Still I would not have Sarah undertake it unless she felt that it was her calling and she could enter upon it in the confidence of divine support. Dear Augustus amid all the changes you have undergone all the havoc that has been made of old superstitions and theological opinions have you preserved a live faith in divine guidance? Do you feel as if there were a power on which to lean, to which to appeal, a Father on whose bosom you could recline, a Mother's love on which you could calculate in all emergencies. I say a mother's love, because the power we call God combines the masculine and feminine natures, or it could not, as it does, minister to *all* of our being. Among the Hindoos [sic] the male and female elements constituted God, that is there were two necessary to creation, so also in Persia and if I mistake not generally among the Heathen. The Jews worshipped one God and as that God was masculine, they exhibit in their character the bold, aggressive, combattive [sic] traits which characterized their Jehovah. They lacked preeminently the feminine traits, and it was to fill up this deficiency that Christ came cloathed with all the gentler virtues, the beautiful embodiment of Love. In the then vicious state of the world, when the animal had the predominance, to have deified a female as the companion of, and inseparably connected with the Divine Being, would have been a slander on the Jehovah of the Jews, but their God did not, could not, never can fill up the necessities of man. The time came when the race demanded something besides power, majesty, glory, and righteousness to satisfy its cravings, and whenever man develops beyond the present, his need is always met and just such a ministration is prepared for him as supplies the newly experienced want. It has been thus with Christ. How my soul revelled in his love, how like a mother to lay down his life. I recur to those seasons even now with gratitude and while my soul is delivered from the dogmas of Christianity I rejoice that my faith in and love to the Supreme has suffered no diminution. But I must stop or I cannot write even a few lines to my dear Sarah. The money I hoped to receive has not been paid and possibly never will be. Yours very affy. S.M.G. . . .

⚘ 7 ⚘

SMG to Augustus Wattles

Dear Augustus,

. . . It is indeed true, that the millenial state which we foresee "requires a greater change in man than it does in woman"—man has not been placed in as favorable a position for spirit growth as woman. He has had power, irresponsible, absolute power, his physical development gave him strength, his animal propensities aided by a strong will naturally led him to subdue and rule over and ride over every being, who was his inferior, woman was in physical power, in intellectual development, she had nothing to draw out the wealth of her mind, but crushed as she was, suffering from the false theology and falser feelings of her brother, she drank to the dregs the cup of woe, regarded as a mere instrument to gratify licentiousness, or to perpetuate the human species, she was of course debased and dishonored, but the feminine element, the *Love* nature grew and flourished notwithstanding, and in the secret places where she watered the earth with her tears . . . sprung up sweet flowers of gentleness, peace, forebearance and mercy. These have grown in the shade of private life, they have bloomed in the garden of Home, where mother, wife, sister, daughter have encircled man with the charities, and given him the sympathies, and breathed around him and into

73

him the spirit of love. Now when after years of preparation amidst sorrow, toil, disgrace and scorn she is prepared to *begin* her mission there are hearts prepared to receive her message, spirits ready to cooperate with her. There is dear, Augustus, a noble band of men, who earnestly desire and are doing all they can, to promote the education of woman. True they are not all equally high up the hill, the view of some is circumscribed by their position, they do not see the expanse of heaven in its length and breadth, but nevertheless they do sincerely desire the emancipation of woman, so far as they see emancipation to be consistent with what to them seems her best welfare. I do not blame them, nor do I blame the past, it was, it is, a necessary part of that baptism of blood, which prepares for great moral enterprizes. All I ask for woman is human Rights, these are in their nature eternal, and sooner or later will be accorded to her, they must regulate themselves. If woman demands, or claims more than is her due as an intellectual and moral being, it will soon be manifest. All I ask of woman is, that she live out her highest nature, cultivate her mental and spiritual powers and be an epistle of Love known and read of all men—this and this alone can rightly open to her the path to excellence and glory, the glory of transforming the Lion into the Lamb. . . .

❧ 8 ❧

SMG, Manuscript Essay:
The Education of Women

In the period 1852–57 Sarah Grimké prepared what she intended to be a major work, a book on the condition of women, to follow up her earlier work, *Letters on the Equality of the Sexes.* She intended to focus on "the disabilities of women" in law, education, marriage and economic status. She never completed this work. Four fragments of essays—"Condition of Women," "Education of Women," "Marriage" and "Sisters of Charity"—and some scattered notes in her diaries are all that are left. There is also a brief essay fragment she entitled "Essay on the Laws Respecting Women" from which I cite passages elsewhere in this book. It is available to the interested reader in Bartlett's *Sarah Grimké.*

While Sarah did not complete the major synthesis of feminist theory of her day which she had attempted, the essays are of great interest. They illuminate the intellectual achievements of a radical feminist thinker and reflect the limitations of such achievement imposed by the conditions under which she lived. Her aim was twofold: to convince enlightened men that the emancipation and equality of women was in their own best interest, and to convince women to struggle for their own emancipation. She undoubtedly intended to bolster her arguments based on religion, which she had developed in her earlier writings, with arguments from history and ethnography. Her limited education and practically nonexistent access to libraries and research sources made this an unattainable goal.

In this essay she surveys the ground covered in her earlier major work with special emphasis on the adverse effects on women of the denial of education. Her use of her own life experience to illustrate this is unusual for her day, when women hesitated to speak publicly of private matters. It is also very moving and pathetic. Her awareness of the limitations of her intellectual life were acute and unsparing. Particularly interesting is the passage in which she deals with the different psychology of boys and girls created by the educational disadvantaging of women. Here her description is way ahead of her time, and she touches upon issues which are still current and unresolved in the late 20th century.

Also noteworthy in this essay are the various passages dealing with marriage and sexuality. Here she clearly anticipates ideas she will work out a few years later in the essay "Marriage." She links the educational deprivation of women to their dependency on marriage as economic support and in turn shows how the ignorance imposed on women renders them helpless when faced with what today we would call sexual abuse. While the theme of woman's right to control the timing and number of her pregnancies was beginning to be argued by feminists and health reformers in the 1850s, none was as sharp and passionate in her argument as was Sarah Grimké. And she was far ahead of her time in tracing the connections of woman's sexual dependency and their economic and educational status.

Her argument for giving women a chance to serve on school boards was equally ahead of its time.

The manuscript consists of text and various clippings, most of them without ascription. Wherever I could identify the source I have done so; where I could not I have left quotation marks to show that it is a citation. Sarah cut and pasted the manuscript and did some editing, but the sequence of several paragraphs is unclear. I have indicated where I moved paragraphs for greater clarity.

§➔§➔§➔

THE EDUCATION OF WOMEN

"Oh could I but unloose my soul . . .
We're sepulch[er]ed alive and want more room"
[Elizabeth Barrett Browning,] *Aurora Leigh*

There is rich instruction to be gained by "unrolling the scroll of history," by reviewing the past patiently, calmly, philosophically. It . . . is impossible to do honor to the present, to make the best use of all the advantages it offers, to appreciate all the facilities for improvement which cluster round us unless we are acquainted with the history of the Past. Nor can we otherwise know how large a debt of gratitude we owe to those, who have preceded us in the conflict of ages. . . .

I have neither lamentation for the *Then* nor denunciation for the *Now*. All I feel is gratitude for the past, cheerful acquiescence in the present, bright hope for the future. In this spirit I come to the contemplation of a subject, so vast that it baffles my powers of comprehension, yet so exacting and imperative that I dare not shrink from it. . . .

Knowledge has ever been the lever which has raised man to a higher state. . . . In all ages, through all the varied experience of individuals and nations, knowledge has been the power which has civilized, elevated and dignified humanity. In those countries where progress has been most rapid, the thirst for knowledge has been most intense. In his childhood man knew no better way to satisfy this thirst than by subduing his fellow man. He taxed his ingenuity to invent engines of destruction and thus strengthened his intellect and enlarged his capacity, not only to work evil, but to work good. The knowledge of evil is absolutely necessary to a growth in goodness; . . . [m]an must pass through the varied experiences of temptation, sin, repentance, and amendment, that he may gain strength by overcoming. . . . Good and evil, as we term them, are not antagonistic. . . . [H]umanity has never achieved a single conquest without the aid of both. Indeed how can she? What adds to moral strength, but grappling with temptation? What gives intellectual power, but a resolute will to overcome the obstacles interposed by ignorance, and by the difficulties, which in some way or other, start up to impede our progress in knowledge? Difficulties [are] strewn much more thickly in the path of woman, than in that of man. If woman is ready to encounter these trials, to test her strength by conflict, shall she plead in vain for higher educational and industrial advantages? Give her the first, she will open for herself access to the second. Already there are thousands who are regarding the subject of Woman's Rights with earnest interest, thousands of . . . liberal minds, whose sympathy strengthens her to press onward in the glorious work of Reformation. And she gratefully accepts the sympathy and cooperation of man, in this, her novel experience of individual, yet conjoint existence and personal responsibility. . . . We should neither be surprised nor daunted at the opposition made to giving woman the same educational advantages as men; it is but a few years since the same spirit rose in sterner rebellion against the laws providing for the education of the masses. . . . The ignorant were as well satisfied with their ignorance, as averse to be roused from their mental atrophy or paralysis as the women are to be roused from their present dependent state.

But the law which furnished the means of improvement to the untaught has proved an incalculable blessing, has unfolded powers which otherwise would have lain dormant, and brought into activity a wealth of intelligence and virtue of more value than the mines of California.* Indeed the loftiest flight of imagination must fail to picture the benefits that have accrued from the passage of that single law. . . . "*General* education imparts general freedom of thought. And this freedom of thought is the parent of vigorous exertion, of self reliance, of that thorough sense of responsibility, which causes every one to walk alertly and yet cautiously over the difficult paths of life."

> But woe to those who trample on the mind
> A deathless thing
> They know not what they do
> Nor what they deal with.
> Man perchance may bind the flower
> His step hath bruised
> Or light anew the torch he quenches
> Or to music wind the lyre string
> From his touch that flew.

* She here refers to the Massachusetts law of 1642 that required every town to maintain a grammar school.

But for the mind Oh tremble and beware
Lay not rude hands on God's dominion there.

There are some faculties appertaining to the human species, which can never be smothered, much less extirpated. They are a part of the many; without them he [man] would no longer be much distinguished from the brute: the first of these is his religious sentiment; the second is his intellectual nature. These constitute his capability of improveability. These preeminently call for cultivation; these make the most powerful appeal to our fellow beings for aid and cooperation, that they may have the best means of producing the highest development. We cannot alter the structure of . . . human understanding, but we can assist in evolving its powers, or we can prevent their expansion by denying them the means adapted to their growth. Females are gifted with powers as susceptible of cultivation as men. Why then should they not have the same facilities and the same inducements for improving their faculties?

Education in its most extensive sense is indissolubly connected with free institutions. Narrow, or circumscribe the limits of one, and you inevitably cripple the other. The tendency of the mind is to progress and whatever widens the avenues of knowledge adds so much strength to our free institutions. . . . Our republic might be enlightened by the study of ancient history. In Egypt "trade was carried on by women, the sculptures represent them buying and selling in the market, and meeting with men at feasts apparently on terms of equality." Champollion found on a doorway representations of Thoth and a feminine divinity, who presided over arts, science and literature.* . . . In Greece women were admitted to the priesthood, enjoyed its highest dignities and were regarded with great veneration; so were the vestal virgins of Rome, who were an order of priestesses. Among the Celtic tribes women were on the same level with men; "both sexes held consultation together in councils of state and fought in battle with equal bravery." The Teutons were remarkable for the respect they showed to women. With them women were on an equality with men in church and state, and were habitually consulted by men in all important affairs, and were their

* Jean-François Champollion (1790–1832), scholar of Egyptian hieroglyphics.

only physicians. Tacitus says, "The Germans suppose some divine and prophetic quality in their women, and are careful neither to disregard their admonitions, nor neglect their answers."**

I do not cite these facts because I regard women as the recipients of the divine afflatus any more than men, but simply to . . . compare the solid advantages enjoyed by heathen women, in having the same opportunities for development and practical usefulness as their brethren, with the blighting system adopted in all Christian nations with respect to the education and practical usefulness of our sex almost from birth to death. . . . Can they [women] develop symmetrically their whole being, when they are deprived of the advantages so lavishly bestowed by church and state upon their brethren?

How many millions are invested in colleges, universities, theological seminaries for the education and exaltation of *men* to prepare them to fill offices of honor, trust, and emolument? Is there one million invested for such purposes for the benefit of women? Nay, they not only are not blest with such patronage, but are even deprived of property by legal enactments, so that they can do very little for themselves. Indeed such is the false estimation of the needs of the sexes, that women are content to labor for the education of men, whilst they themselves sit down in *commendable* ignorance. How many girls have been united in sewing societies to educate young men for the ministry, nor dreamed that the intellectual feast prepared by their industry for others, was . . . really a need of their own minds. . . . I received a letter from Vermont in which the writer deplores the erroneous view which consigned herself and her sisters to comparative ignorance and poverty, while the sons of the family had college educations and were prospering in their several callings. The father's means being slender, his wife and daughters endured many privations that the young men might be supported at college, confidently believing that they would share the benefits conferred by their sufferings; but alas! the young men left college, married, set up for themselves and at the death of the father the widow and daughters were compelled to toil on for a bare subsistence. Had they been educated, this would not have been so. Cases like this are numerous. Suffer me then to entreat that you will not close against woman the schools of learning and science, thus shutting out the light from

** Cornelius Tacitus (A.D. 56?–125?), Roman historian.

those whom God committed to your guardianship at the creation, by endowing you with superior physical strength. In the past you have nobly fulfilled your trust—you have shielded her in war; in seasons of peril you have thrown your bodies around her as a rampart, and sought safety for her at your own cost. But in the private life how is it? The existing laws can answer that she is your slave, the victim of your passions, the sharer willingly and unwillingly of your licentiousness. It is to save you, as well as her, from the gratification of unbridled desires, to open for you both a glorious path to happiness and usefulness, that I long to see her qualified to fill the station of wife and of mother.

Mother! Is aught so sacred? Is it strange that "the Hindoos regarded with holy reverence the great mystery of human birth"? Were they impure thus to regard it? or are we impure that we do not so regard it? A reverence for the mystery of birth, a feeling, that the means by which this wonderful event is produced ought to be held sacred, would go far to inspire human beings with a love of chastity and to give to one sex self-control, to the other the proprietorship of her own person, and to bring into existence a race of beings who would be welcomed at their entrance into life with a mother's love and joy, and a father's blessing, and whose inheritance would be health of body, strength, and elasticity of mind. . . .

Forgive me, if I intrude upon you a chapter of my personal experience. With me learning was a passion, and under more propitious circumstances, the cultivation of my mind would have superseded every other desire. In vain I entreated permission to go hand in hand with my brothers through their studies. The only answer to my earnest pleadings was "You are a girl—what do you want with Latin and Greek etc.? You can never use them," accompanied sometimes by a smile, sometimes by a sneer. Had I received the education I coveted and been bred to the profession of the law, a dignity to which I secretly aspired, I might have been a useful member of society, and instead of myself and my property being taken care of I might have been a protector of the helpless and the unfortunate, a pleader for the poor and the dumb.

> Back useless tears, back to your native spring.
> Your tributary drops might calm less bitter woes
> But for an aimless life there is no balm. . . .

The reason why women effect so little and are so shallow is because their aims are low. Marriage is the prize for which they strive. If failed in that, they rarely rise above the disappointment. Their life blood is curdled and hence they become useless. . . . ."

My nature thus denied her appropriate nutriment, her course counteracted, her aspirations crushed, found relief in another direction—painting, poetry, general reading, largely interspersed with words of imagination and tales of fiction largely occupied my time, but still I longed for an education which would prepare me for future usefulness. At gay fifteen I was ushered into fashionable life; there I fluttered a few brief years, my better nature all the while rising in insurrection against the course I was pursuing, teaching me to despise myself and those who surrounded me in this pageant existence. Ofttimes as I glittered in the ball room has my soul been awakened from its witching slumber by the solemn query "What doest thou; where are the talents committed to thy charge?" These intrusive thoughts were however soon silenced by the approach of some trifler, by the call to join the festive dance, and I drowned my remorse and my hopeless desires in thoughtless conversations. But for my tutelary god, my idolized brother, my young passionate nature, stimulated by that love of admiration, which carries with terrific swiftness many a high and noble nature down the stream of folly to the whirlpool of an unhallowed marriage, I had rushed into this life long misery. I cannot even now look back to those wasted years without a blush of shame at this prostitution of my womanhood, without a feeling of agony at this utter perversion of the needs of my being.

Happily for me this butterfly life did not last long; my ardent nature had another channel opened through which it rushed with its wonted impetuosity. Yielding to the importunities of an elderly friend I went to hear Dr. Kollock of Savannah preach; went, not to hear from his lips the glad tidings of salvation, but that my ear might be gratified with his ravishing eloquence. He described in his own touching, exquisite, powerful language the character of Christ, his tenderness, his yearning compassion, his surpassing love. My whole being was taken captive. I made a full and free surrender and vowed eternal fealty to Jesus. To manifest my sincerity, in my zeal I burnt my paintings, destroyed my little library of poetry and fiction and gave to the flames my gay apparel. I may not proceed with this sad history of the squandering of powers, which if rightly cultivated might have saved on the one hand from vanity and folly, and on the other from superstitious terror and irrational fanaticism; might have made me worthy of the name of woman, a temple meet for divinity to dwell in. I might have been an intelligent Christian, not a blind and delirious devotee wending my agonized steps over a pathway of darkness and bitter experiences which almost dethroned reason. . . . Again I say forgive me this brief notice of myself. I was tempted to give it, because I believe that my sorrows are not uncommon sorrows. . . . Many a woman shudders as she takes a retrospect of life at the terrible eclipse of those intellectual powers, which in early life seemed prophetic of usefulness and happiness, hence the army of martyrs among married and unmarried women, who not having cultivated a taste for science, art, or literature form a corps of nervous patients who make fortunes for agreeable physicians and idols of their clergymen.

The time has come for these secret breathings to be heard. The projection of the idea of Human Rights is only the irrepressible protest of reason through woman against her present position. . . . Let us redeem ourselves from the degradation which has been the natural consequence of woman's having been regarded a mere instrument to be used for the gratification of passion, as the upper servant in the domestic relations of man to keep things comfortable for her lord, to prepare, or have prepared his food and clothing to produce a pair of slippers to put on when alas! he's weary and to nurse *his* babies. I may not say *hers*, for too often she has not been a willing partner to their birth, for she has felt that the rapid multiplication of children imposed upon her duties she was wholly unfit to perform. With shattered health and soured temper, and self control swept away by this over taxation of her physical powers, she has found it impossible to fill acceptably the station of wife and mother. The uncongenial pair have been frequently held together because divorce under our existing laws, which often deprive a woman of her children, inflicts more agony. . . .

/Does not the paucity of food for reflection in the pursuits of women in times past furnish us a sufficient answer to the query, Why are they inferior? They have been unable to bring into exercise their intellectual powers because they have had no field for the practical application of the knowledge they acquired. Hence the habit of reflection has been rarely and parsimoniously produced in them.

The present has been justly called the age of physical civilization. ... Physical civilization lies at the foundation of all higher civilization./* It constitutes the rudiments of moral and intellectual civilization—and the immense progress in this direction offers a hope of redemption for women from those slavish and absorbing occupations which have devoured their time and stunted their intellect. ... Women are becoming wearied with the everlasting round of domestic labor, and they hail with gratitude and joy every thing that promises to relieve them from constant revolution round the cauldron and the kettle.

Until women are thoro'ly educated they stand in a false position to society and are a dead weight on the government under which they live. Nothing can render them otherwise, but the "full development of their intellectual, as well as active faculties. ..."

Inequalities and injustice in any government naturally produce dissatisfaction and suspicion. In a democracy, these feelings are greatly strengthened and increased by the superior intelligence of the people, for intelligence quickens the perception of wrong and greatly increases the suffering which arises from a sense of oppression. ... Freedom and equality furnish a salutary discipline for the mind and open a vast field to intellectual effort. They strengthen and preserve the power, independence, acuteness, originality and elasticity of the mind, which can never become palsied, so long as it interests itself in Human Rights. Education furnishes the means for extensive information and widens the bounds of human experience, which embraces the past and the present.

It is doubtless the feeling of injury on the part of woman which has induced a few of us to claim the Rights so unjustly withheld. It is because we feel that we have powers which are crushed, responsibilities which we are not permitted to exercise, duties which we are not prepared to fulfil, rights vested in us as moral and intellectual beings, which are utterly ignored and trampled upon. It is because

---

* The preceding section, set off by slashes, was crossed out in the manuscript.

we feel this so keenly that we now demand an equal education with man, to qualify us to be coworkers with him in the great drama of human life. . . . We come filled with a sense of the moral sublimity of our present position . . . to demand as equals, in the name of Him who created us our appropriate place in the scale of humanity. Marvel not that so few have joined our band. The mightiest river drops a little streamlet from the mountain's side, the most stupendous mountain is gathered grain by grain. . . . But two, or three were gathered together at the first meeting of our revolutionary fathers, but fifty-six signed the Declaration of Independence. Nevertheless, the grand and glorious words had been uttered "Liberty or Death," "Taxation and Representation" and they rang through the land with magic power. . . . Will it not be so with the words which woman utters? Rights, Equality, Education, Self-support, and Representation. . . .

Can we marvel that woman does not immediately realize the dignity of her own nature, when we remember that she has been so long used as a means to an end, and that end the comfort and pleasure of man, regarded as his *property*, a being created for his benefit, and living like a parasite on *his* vitality. When we remember how little her intellect has been taken into account in estimating her value in society, and that she received as truth the dogma of her inferiority? . . .

The conflict of interests and opinions between the sexes cannot fail to create antagonistic feelings, and this will necessarily be felt in all their relations to each other. This conflict arises from withholding rights on one side and the injury sustained from this injustice on the other. Perhaps there is nothing that will tend so rapidly and so powerfully to the equalization of the sexes as similar educational advantages. Education opens new theatres of action, furnishes new incentives to exertion. It gives the mind a just appreciation of itself, enables it to estimate its influence in society, and introduces it into new trains of reflection, and new habits of thought. True, education does not transform men or women into angels, but it goes further than anything else to lessen vice, and is a constant counterpoise to idleness and frivolity. . . .

The fellow feeling which universal education produces among a people is clearly discernible in America, and its influence in strengthening that sympathy is incalculable. When learning in all its higher branches shall become the common property of both sexes; when the girl, as well as the boy, may anticipate with earnest delight the complete course of study, which will enable her to look forward to a life of continued culture, of independence and of the fulfilment of high and honorable trusts, the contemplation of such a future will raise her ideas of herself beyond the ephemeral sphere of fashion, or the toilsome drudgery of that incessant manual labor, which is calculated in most cases to stultify intellect and which may be performed for a small compensation by those who have hands but are nearly destitute of brains. It would be as wise to set an accomplished lawyer to saw wood as a business as to condemn an educated and sensible woman to spend all her time in boiling potatoes and patching old garments. Yet this is the lot of many a one, who incessantly stitches, and boils, and bakes, compelled to thrust back out of sight the aspirations which fill her soul. Think not because I thus speak, that I would withdraw woman from the duties of domestic life, far from it; let her fulfil in the circle of home all the obligations that rest upon her, but let her not waste her powers on inferior objects when higher and holier responsibilities demand her attention.

It is for the production of the highest civilization that my spirit yearns, but the highest civilization can never exist in all its beauty and fulness, unless the opportunities for education are the same for both sexes. Equality is the most powerful and the most efficient means of bringing mind to act upon mind, and this action and reaction stimulates and elevates, purifies and deepens thought power. . . .

The common school system of education which was adopted in New England when the colony consisted of only a few thousands is now established nearly all over the United States, and there can be no doubt that it has contributed, more than any single institution, to the advancement of the people in arts and manufactures, in commerce and literature, in morality and religion, and has been the prolific parent of innumerable blessings. Just in proportion as this system prevails and is carried out on the liberal principle of equality, just in that proportion will civilization increase.

Among the most extraordinary and flagrant violations of the spirit of Republicanism is the exclusion of women from school committees, altho' the schools are composed of daughters, as well as sons. It would be extremely difficult to repress the feeling of indignation at this ignoring of the feeling and rights of woman, if I did not clearly see that it originated from circumstances over which neither sex could exercise any control. In the early settlement of every country, the men greatly outnumber the women, school houses are often at a distance from most of the dwellings of the pupils' parents, the access to them is difficult, and women with families and few conveniences to aid in domestic labor are too busy and too much worn from fatigue to attend to any thing but the immediate duties of home. This is now no longer the case. Women can afford the time, quite as well as men, and their judgment, their sympathy, their maternal care is needed in all such committees. That they have abundant leisure to attend to this important duty, is manifest from the fact that they devote so much time to benevolent associations, none of which have so strong a claim upon them as the sacred duty of examining and ascertaining the qualifications and character of those to whom is entrusted the care of their children. . . . "But," said a gentleman, "you cannot find women fit to put on such committees." I shall not stop to disprove this assertion, but simply state, that I have known committee *men*, who certainly were more unfit for their business than any *women* who would be likely to be placed in that position, because unusual care would be taken in the selection of women, as is always the case in the introduction of any innovation. We have, moreover, an admirable provision in human nature, conservatism, which prevents change from being brought about too rapidly. The love of old usages exercises a sort of guardianship over society, somewhat resembling the tutelage of a parent over a child. It is a salutary check to the headlong rush of youthful feeling. And as many parents find it difficult to recognize the manhood and womanhood of their children, albeit they are sometimes far ahead of them in clear sightedness as to what will be most conducive to their own benefit, so conservatism is very slow to acknowledge that any proposed amendment in the structure of society will be really beneficial. . . .

We cannot easily foresee what will be the result of placing men and women on an equality in education. One thing however is certain, it will be an unspeakable advantage to society. The community must increase in wisdom and strength, in proportion to the diffusion of learning, since there is nothing more admirably calculated to strengthen individual character than the unlimited expansion of knowledge. In a popular government this is of paramount importance, because intelligence and cultivation tend more than anything else, to qualify the elect to act with judgment and benevolence, and the electors to judge of the fitness of those who are proposed as candidates for office, so that all the truly valuable institutions of the country will rest upon a firmer basis. We appeal then to the States in which we live to incorporate us among her citizens; to give us the same advantages she gives to her sons; to open to us the portals of science, art and literature. We ask them to extend to us the liberality they have so generously manifested to our brethren. Judge and condemn us not, until you have placed within our reach the intellectual advantages which those among the other sex, least susceptible to improvement, can command at will; whilst we are compelled to stand without and plead in vain for admission. But, it will be enquired, why we desire an extended education, since we already have what is sufficient for all the duties of woman's narrow sphere. What is the use of higher educational privileges, when there is no field for the exercise of our powers, after we have spent years in their cultivation. First, we ask education as a means to an end; that end, is greater fitness to fulfil our duties in all the domestic and social relations. There can be no attainment too high, no learning too profound, not to be advantageously turned to account in the sacred circle of Home. Second, we ask it, because we covet an enlarged sphere of usefulness; we feel a thirst for improvement which can only be quenched by drinking freely of the streams of knowledge. Third, we ask it, because we feel as if the time had come, when God having awakened new desires and stirred within us new aspirations, was calling upon us to aid with all our powers in promoting the progress of the race. To God, to the cause of Humanity, we desire to consecrate ourselves, and we ask your aid. Will you give it to us cheerfully, lovingly, as we have given ours to you? How many toilsome hours have we spent to enable the poor, but aspiring youth, to obtain an education? Our contributions have been small, but we have bestowed them rejoicingly, faithfully, to prepare some of our brethern for usefulness and duty. Yes, there are many men now filling stations of honor and of profit, whose education and success have been purchased by the ceaseless toil of their mothers, sisters, and female friends. We speak not boastingly, we simply state facts. Fourth, we ask an education, because we believe that it will exalt and purify woman and will enlarge her means of happiness, and because we know that there is a guarantee in woman's nature that she will never forsake those duties and enjoyments in which are centered her supreme felicity. . . .

To institute a comparison between the sexes savors neither of justice nor common sense, because the advantages of the one have been, and are so vastly superior to those of the other. If we wish to ascertain the capability of woman for improvement, let us compare the women of the present century with the women of two hundred years ago. The number of those who pursue science, literature, and art are ten if not an hundred fold what they were during the later part of the 17th century.

It is no longer a matter of speculation, but an established fact, that in proportion as education becomes the common property of a people, in that proportion crime lessens. The register of crimes testifies to this. If then the diffusion of the elements of education produces such blessed effects, is it not clear that to give to such women as desire it, and can devote themselves to literary and scientific pursuits, all the advantages enjoyed by men of the same class, will lessen essentially the number of thoughtless, idle, vain and frivolous women, and thus secure to society, the services of those who now hang as dead weight on the family and the community? The number of those indeed is already lessened, for women have shared, to some extent, in the general diffusion of knowledge, through the common school system. The multiplication of newspapers and periodicals, the rapid increase of which is one of the most remarkable features in the history of our country, has also greatly enlarged their means of information. . . .

It is not from women who are reclining in the lap of opulence and splendor, and eating the bread of idleness, that we can expect aid; they have all they are capable of enjoying, nor ask a better lot. Reformists have almost universally arisen among what are termed the inferior classes of society. They are not so steeped in the enjoyment of material delights as to be unable to appreciate moral and intellectual pleasures. They are not unfitted by luxury and selfish indulgence from casting their eyes over the condition of society and pondering the best means of advancing the happiness and prosperity of the race. . . . [T]hose who feel the daily calamity of unjust laws, the degradation of being in an inferior and abnormal position, whose souls are on fire because of oppression and imprisonment, these are the men and women who awaken public attention to the needed reformation. . . . I am greatly mistaken if the time has not past [sic] when women listened with astonishment to the wisdom of their brethren, and concluded that they alone were the repositories of knowledge, and the only part a woman had to perform was to listen in mute wonder to the gracious words which dropped from their lips. Women have conceived the bold design of scaling the heights of knowledge, and possessing themselves of the inestimable riches concealed behind the ramparts. Riches of which they have heard, but which they have been sedulously instructed were beyond their reach, and around which a flaming sword continually moved. They are not stirred by envy, or jealousy, but are stimulated by an insatiable desire for progress, by a deathless hope of usefulness, and it is by being elevated to the same level with man that they see the means of accomplishing these anticipations.

There is unquestionably in this day, more than at any preceding period, a willingness to hear and consider the various opinions now afloat touching the great interests of humanity. . . . Dissatisfaction with the state of society marks the present era. This feeling should never be disregarded for it is the daughter of Suffering, the mother of Reformation. Whatever may have given rise to it, it demands our sympathy and is entitled to a respectful hearing—rudely and unfeelingly, carelessly and sneeringly to thrust aside any who ask modestly and earnestly for a redress of grievances, is certainly unmanly and unchristian. To visit upon the petitioners the follies and the vices of a portion of the class with which they are identified is cruel. To deny them relief because they are dragging a tremendous weight of ignorance, idleness, fashion, helplessness and frivolity, is ungenerous. . . .

The thought of the equality of the sexes is no man's invention, "but the rising of the general tide in the human soul." This idea is itself an epoch; that it is so fully accepted by a few individuals, as to stir them to remonstrance and to action, to union and mutual communication of opinions, feelings and views is a commanding fact. "Revolutions go not backward. There is no good now enjoyed by society that was not once problematical." An idea built the wall of separation between the sexes, and an idea will crumble it to dust. . . .

One consideration . . . I must place before the reader . . . viz.:, the effect necessarily produced on girls and boys by the different prospects which their future presents. The boy, as soon as he is capable of thinking, feels that he has to be a worker, that he is to stand on his own feet and exercise his talents in some profitable business. His self-respect, his love of independence, are at once healthfully excited. He feels himself an individual being, draws in with every breath, at home, at school, in the social circle, the idea of self-reliance and self-support. Hence, his efforts to prepare himself for this unavoidable business of life are powerfully stimulated. His studies, though often irksome and ill suited to his taste, are pursued as a means to an end, and thus he is constantly and urgently pushed onward in the career of learning. It is not so with girls. They study under the paralysing idea that their acquirements can never be brought into practical use; they may subserve the purposes of promoting individual pleasure, domestic and social enjoyment in conversation. But what are they in comparison with the grand stimulation of independence and self reliance and of the capability of contributing to the comfort and happiness of those whom they love as their own souls? Many a talented and highly educated girl feels no pleasure in looking beyond her school life, because she sees no bright and useful future beyond. Delighted as she is with the acquisition of knowledge, she yet sends forth the plaintive inquiry, What shall I do? My learning can purchase for me neither independence, nor the ability to minister to the wants of others. My food, my raiment are not the product of my own industry. Shall this touching appeal meet with no response in the hearts of fathers, brothers, husbands and sons? . . .

❧ 9 ❧

SMG to Harriot Hunt

After her brief stay in Boston and in Washington, D.C., and her unsuccessful efforts to set herself up independently of the Weld family, Sarah Grimké had returned to the family in 1853, resigned to continuing with them as before. It was not until the summer of 1854 that the family moved to the cooperative settlement of Raritan Bay Union in New Jersey. There, Theodore Weld was the director of the school and Angelina and Sarah taught various subjects. Sarah was unhappy with this move; she could not adjust to communitarian life even after several years. She mostly taught French and derived little satisfaction from her teaching, whereas both Weld and Angelina enjoyed teaching. In this letter she expresses her feelings quite openly and without the attitude of resignation which had characterized so much of her domestic life in her sister's household.

The letter is remarkable also for its free tone of love and intimacy, something quite lacking in Sarah Grimké's correspondence. In fact, the phrase "Beloved" seldom occurs in her correspondence. (See Doc. 10, where she uses it to address Sarah Wattles, whom she regarded as a niece and surrogate daughter.) I do not think it carries any erotic connotation in this case, but it does denote unusual intimacy and spontaneity. Sarah had many women friends and correspondents, but Dr. Harriot Hunt was the only woman to whom she

looked up and who could counsel her. The two women seldom met
in person, since Dr. Hunt lived in Boston, and Sarah traveled infre-
quently. Harriot Hunt reciprocated Sarah's friendship and affection;
in her autobiography she expressed her admiration for her as "a rare
and true woman" in dedicating the book to her.*

§➡§➡§➡

Eagleswood School, May 23 [1855]

A glorious day this my precious Harriot a day that makes me think
of Eden when Creation all fresh and beautiful sprung from its mak-
ers hands and every leaf and every bud and every blossom was re-
dolant of love and beauty. If you had been with me this morning
when I was inhaling the balmy fragrance of the early day you would
have enjoyed it. I am too sorry you have no daguerotype [sic] of
this place on your mind, but all in good time if we remain here. I
do not know that I ever lived on any place where the surroundings
were such a fascination to my spirit, or perhaps I should say to my
love of the beautiful, every ramble thro' the woods, or along the
shore, presents new charms, and the ever varying face of the bay is
a source of ceaseless enjoyment, while the sound of its waves sometimes dashing impetuously, sometimes murmuring softly as the summer breeze, fill the eye the ear the heart with wonder and delight—
sometime we may possibly sit together here and also at Niagara and
adore in silent reverence The God who made them all. Harriot, how

* Harriot Kezia Hunt (1805–1875), together with her sister Sarah,
trained with British homeopathic physicians and set up a medical practice
in Boston in 1835. They concentrated on diet, natural healing methods and
attention to mental and psychological problems and achieved good results
with many patients given up by regular physicians. Her sister left the practice upon her marriage, but Harriot Hunt continued it until 1873, combin-
ing it with lectures to women on physiology and healthy living. She twice
applied for admission to Harvard Medical school, but was refused. The
Female Medical College of Philadelphia awarded her an honorary degree
of Doctor of Medicine in 1853. She was active in the woman's rights movement and for two decades withheld her taxes in protest over woman's dis-
franchisement.

do human beings live without the religious element—where is the deepest joy of the heart, but in the exercise of the worship element, in the recognition of a Father's imprint on all around us. . . .

It seems to me the Medical profession opens more than all other things a highway of improvement to woman. It is peculiarly her sphere to minister to the sick, it affords such an extensive field to physiological research to an investigation of all that pertains to the structure and uses of our organs—to the injury sustained by those organs from the abuses to which they are subjected. It will bring women into such intimate relations with families, afford such an opportunity of knowing the true condition of men and women in the marriage relation and let them into those secrets which must be known and canvassed in order to be remedied—what an unspeakable blessing it will be to the world, if women of the right stamp, women of strong mind and acquainted or capable of becoming acquainted with the science of medecine [sic] are spread broadcast over the land. But in addition to talent and strength there must be Love; no woman can justly fulfill her mission as a physician without a love spirit, this alone can bring us into unity and internal correspondence with those with whom we are in outward communications and no woman deserves the name of physician who cannot hold intercourse with the spirits of her patients and minister to the higher nature. Hence I fear nothing more, than that women unblest with this gift and whose highest attainment is a scientific knowledge of medicine should crowd into the profession. I have not yet seen one who has passed through the colleges who comes up to my beau ideal of a physician, but my knowledge is limited as to number and slight as to any intimate acquaintance. Ann Preston strikes me as the best.

. . . I sometimes indulge the hope that the monotony of our life may give place to some other phase and that as it seems impossible for us to continue the school here next year Theodore may consent to take a year's rest and have a little time to relax from the positive state, I am persuaded that to live a life of such tension as he lives is utterly antagonistic to the symmetrical development of the moral being. The family relation is almost inevitably broken up, and the best and holiest feelings of our nature being denied their natural play are blighted, choked overwhelmed and frittered away by the endless appeals to feeling, sympathy, firmness which necessarily occur in a boarding school. The future is all a blank. Mr. Spring is in

New York, but his children are sick and it is altogether uncertain when he will get out here and unless he can obtain $50,000 at least to endow the school and make the necessary improvements and build a wharf etc., it seems to me that this must be a failure. However time will make its own developments and I feel no anxiety about the future. For a little while I was in a sort of extacy [*sic*] at the idea of getting away from this place, for notwithstanding the beauty of the scenery, it is not the home of my heart. I dragged my material part hither because the attraction of the children was irresistible and I rejoice that I came, though Theodore says I have been cross all the time. To be honest I have turned out much worse than I expected—trials have chafed me and perceiving, as I think, that the labor, money, wear and tear of body, soul and spirit has all been made to accomplish a false idea, it has taken more patience than I possessed to meet the treading on toes, hustling with elbows, striking sharp corners which such near proximity produced—but I have had a valuable tho' hard experience and trust the discipline will not be quite useless. I must say T. and A. have borne themselves nobly under the disappointments and trials we have had—as for me I have been too indignant to behave well.

I should greatly have enjoyed your discussion with H. Mann, he will not help the cause of woman greatly, but his strenuous efforts to educate her will do a greater work than he anticipates. Prepare woman for duty and usefulness and she will laugh at any boundaries man may set for her when she is endued [endowed] with power from on high she will as naturally fall into her right position as the feather floats in the air, as the pebble sinks in the water. . . . Beloved, when we meet we shall rest on each other's hearts. . . . Yours ever in love S. M. G.

❧ 10 ❧

SMG to Sarah Wattles

The following letter written to Sarah Wattles, the young daughter of her friends Augustus and Susan, is of interest primarily because it expresses Sarah's thoughts about marriage in a private communication. The correspondence of her ideas in this letter with the text of the essay "Marriage" (Doc. 11) reinforces the authentication of that essay and its ascription to Sarah Grimké. As an "interested observer of domestic life," Sarah expresses her disillusionment with the institution of marriage, hinting not only at the human foibles which make living together difficult, but at "the difference of situation" [of husband and wife]. But the primary cause of marital difficulty is too frequent child bearing. It is a theme she will expand on in her essays "Marriage" and "Sisters of Charity."

Sarah looked upon Sarah Wattles as an adopted niece or surrogate daughter. Here she somewhat pathetically expresses her hopes that Sarah would use her talents to carry on her, Sarah Grimké's, work. "I wanted to add another jewel to my crown." [This is a reference to her effort to write another book.] Now she is resigned that she cannot do that, but "I have a chastened, joyous feeling that any jewel will sparkle on the brow of Kansas and radiate a light there which is perhaps more needed than it is here." Sarah Wattles lived in Kansas.

§❧§❧§❧

Eagleswood School Aug. 12th [1855]

My precious Sarah:

How rejoiced and thankful I am that you feel so contented and hopeful in your present situation, that Kansas feels like a Home to you, any where may be a paradise if we can realize the idea of Home. Your letters evince such a spirit of contentment, such a resolution to look on the bright side of the picture, that I anticipate for you as much happiness as is the ordinary lot of mortals and I have long made up my mind that with rare exceptions every human being enjoys more than he suffers. I cannot take the sombre view of life that many do, viz. that you have only a choice of evils. It seems to me there is much positive pleasure, though all happiness connected with material objects has its accompanying cares, and in this arrangement of Providence I see infinite wisdom, for the very care often enhances the enjoyment. Take for instance married life, the only normal state for man, because the only state in which the highest affections of our nature can find a sufficient field for growth. What a multiplicity of cares cluster round domestic life. How the husband has to toil for the wife, and the wife for the husband and both for the children, yet what married persons would exchange the cares and labors and enjoyments of marriage for the barrenness of single life. I think I know something of these two states, although I have never been married, for I have suffered for, and delighted in Angelina's children as much almost as she has, and you know I was so covetous that I wanted to add another jewel to my crown, but Heavenly Father said, No, so I acquiesced, though the disappointment was not small and now I have a chastened, joyous feeling that my jewel will sparkle on the brow of Kansas and radiate a light there which is perhaps more needed than it is here. Yes my Sarah in the mild lustre of your virtues I anticipate much for your home circle, much for your social environments. You know I do not mean to flatter, but I do mean to awaken you to a keener sense of responsibility, if need be, for the gifts committed to your care. Now that I have stumbled almost unconsciously on the subject of marriage—Let me say a few words as sapiently as if I knew all about it. Well dear Sarah nearly all my life I have been an interested observer of domestic life and came to the theatre of observation with high ideas of family happiness. My *beau* ideal was soon demolished, I found husbands and wives generally disappointed in each other, too much had been expected of human nature, too little allowance made for those traits which the . . . days of courtship . . . did not develop. If the love was disinterested all naturally appeared pleasant, and without any intention to deceive they seemed to each other different from what they really were. If selfishness was the motive which induced the connection, of course great pains were taken to conceal every thing disagreeable, hence lovers really know little of each other unless previous intimacy has brought them into near social relations, and even then large allowance must be made for the vast increase of trials and the difference of situation, which inevitably develops traits perhaps unkown even to the individual. Oh how often I have seen the cup of connubial happiness embittered, or dashed away by daily unamiableness about trifles. [I]n one case the husband liked very much to have mush for his breakfast, his wife did not fancy it and never would have it prepared, these are the little foxes which spoil the tender vines of human happiness. But one of the most fruitful sources of wretchedness in married life is having children so fast that the woman is incapable of doing her duty to them, her temper is fretted, her health broken, and instead of being a help meet, she becomes a burden, the consciousness of this irritates her nerves and some of the loveliest dispositions are transformed into *fretful* exacting and discontented tempers. I hope dear child that you will marry and my earnest prayer is that you may marry wisely—look at the object of your affections through the eye of true love. See that *Principle* is his polar star, that for this we would suffer and die, and the advice of a father to his daughter is not to be despised: "In the choice of a companion, choose a man of aimiable [sic] disposition; religion comes and goes, but temper is there every day." Now, beloved, though I desire to see you blest with the highest blessing of wh[ich] we are susceptible, I should grudge you to the noblest man until you are more matured in mind, more consolidated in physical strength, better qualified to form a judgment on this vital subject—as you have never hinted at any attachment, I may fairly conclude that you are free, and if so that you will be better able to give aunt Sarah's suggestions a place. I do not ask you to take the slightest notice of this subject in writing to me for I have not the remotest desire to lure you to confidence, but to tell you the truth I have long felt anxious lest you should too soon quit the paternal roof. Now I have run on so about "connubial bliss" etc. that my paper is full. Forgive me I will try to do better next time. How shall I thank you for your dear long letter all its details were so interesting, favor me with another soon. . . . Farewell, I will try to write soon again Yours in tender love S.M.G.

❧ 11 ❧

A Problem of Ascription

(GERDA LERNER)

The authorship of the essay "Marriage" cannot be firmly established beyond a reasonable doubt, although I believe it was written by Sarah Grimké. The best I can do is to present all the evidence and explain my reasons for my conviction that Sarah Grimké is the author.

When I first worked in the WELD MSS in 1962 the manuscript was uncatalogued and only roughly divided by periods. The letters of the sisters and of Theodore Weld were not separated, and there was no index. The diaries of Sarah and Angelina and the various notebooks with essay fragments were boxed together. The text of the essay entitled "Marriage" was found among several similar notebooks, filled with essays, all written and some signed by Sarah Grimké, in a box marked with her name. I accepted that ascription, which I believed to have been made on the basis of handwriting, when I first reprinted it in my source collection *The Female Experience* in 1977.

Later that year I received a letter from Professor Carl Degler of Stanford University, informing me that a student of his had seen the manuscript and that now it had been assigned to Angelina Grimké on the basis of the handwriting. Disturbed by this information, I spent considerable time going over photo copies of the manuscript and comparing the handwriting with that of the sisters in letters written roughly in the period 1850–60. On the basis of my lay judgment, that of a historian but not of a graphology expert, I then came to the conclusion that the essay copy in the WELD MSS was indeed *written* by Angelina Grimké. However, contextual evidence convinced me that the *author* is Sarah Grimké. It may be that Angelina had copied an essay written by Sarah. In an age in which all writing and copying was done by hand, people living together often helped each other out that way, and the sisters certainly had done that at times. But there is no positive supporting evidence that this happened in this case. It may also be that the sisters collaborated on this essay and then assigned it to one or the other to write out, the way they did on their earlier articles and letters (see, e.g., Doc. 1). Should that have been the case, authorship could not be definitely established.

When one has read the work of two authors for years and read the formal and informal product of their thought, one develops a sense of each person's style. I felt certain that Sarah was the author on stylistic grounds. She had, as I have noted, both a formal, heavily biblical style and a sharp, incisive informal style. It is the latter she used in this essay. Still, I wanted to be more sure of my case. I went back over the sisters' correspondence during the decade of the 1850s. During that period most of the letters now in the WELD manuscript were written by Sarah. There is no good explanation for this, other than that Angelina's letters may, for some reason, not have survived. In her extant letters, Angelina does not write about working on essays, except one essay on dress reform, which was printed under her name. Sarah makes several references in her correspondence to the fact that Angelina is working on that essay and on various addresses to woman's rights conventions. All of those addresses were printed under Angelina's name. On the other hand, during this period Sarah wrote to all her correspondents that she was working on a series of essays; that she was preparing to write another book, and that she was studying various pertinent subjects in order to do so.

In 1978, I corresponded with Professor Degler at length and sent him, as I did the archivist at the William L. Clements Library, passages from "Sisters of Charity" and from "Education of Women" which seemed to me to match certain passages in "Marriage." The archivist, John C. Dann, agreed with me, and promised to "recatalog the item indicating that the essay is by Sarah Grimké although it is copied in Angelina Grimké's hand." When I returned to the archives in 1996 I found that the entire correspondence regarding this matter, letters from myself and from Professor Degler, were now filed with the manuscript in question. But I failed to convince Professor Degler of my point of view. He wrote me in a letter dated April 3, 1978, which I am quoting with his permission, that he felt Angelina "as the married woman" was the author. He continued:

> . . . what convinces me the essay on "Marriage" is written by Angelina is not its references to male lust or such things, as you suggest in the copy of a page you enclosed in your letter, but the acceptance of sexuality of women. It just seems difficult for me to believe that a woman who was neither married nor a physician would have had such views. I know that Elizabeth Blackwell did, but she also treated many married women and thus learned of women's sexual feelings in marriage and in intercourse as Sarah would not have. . . . [A]t bottom that is the explanation for my feeling that the author is Angelina and not Sarah.

I disagreed with this view. In the 1850s, as several of the documents in this collection show, Sarah Grimké was corresponding frequently and intimately with Dr. Harriot Hunt of Boston, her best friend. She used sexual and medical terms quite openly in her correspondence with Dr. Hunt and even discussed prostitution with her. It seems to me significant that it was she, not Angelina, who discussed Angelina's painful prolapsed uterus with Dr. Hunt and asked for recommendations for a cure. The essay "Marriage" obliquely refers precisely to the situation which Sarah observed in Angelina, when she saw her sister's promising speaking career, which she herself had done so much to foster, brought to an end and her sister incapacitated for much of her married life as a result of a miscarriage and gynecological ailments brought on by too frequent childbirths. The ambivalence Angelina felt in regard to the effect of marriage upon her is expressed in her refusal to seek medical help for her condition at a time when such medical help was readily available in New York and Philadelphia. Sarah wrote to Harriot Hunt that "delicacy" had prevented Angelina from seeking medical help for her condition. It seems unlikely that a woman with too much "delicacy" to seek medical help for herself would write about sexuality in an essay.

Sarah Grimké closely followed the married lives of several younger friends and former students. She corresponded with Dr. Hunt on various medical matters with great frankness. More than half of the ideas expressed in "Marriage" appear in other of her writings. All the "taboo" subjects—sexuality, lust, prostitution, masturbation—were part of her preoccupation during this period, in preparation for her writing a comprehensive text on women's situation. Their appearance in this essay seems perfectly consistent with this preoccupation. On the other hand, there is no evidence of Angelina Grimké pursuing any of these interests in the 1850s.

For all of the above reasons, I felt satisfied that I could stand behind the statement with which I opened this note: the manuscript "Marriage" in the WELD MSS at the Clements library is in Angelina Grimké's handwriting, but for stylistic and larger contextual reason it seems to me to have been authored by Sarah Grimké. Professor Degler, although he still believed it more likely to have been written by Angelina, stated in his book, *At Odds*: "It is not clear which of the sisters, Angelina or Sarah, actually wrote the essay. It is in the hand of Angelina, but the ideas seem to be Sarah's." In a footnote he indicated that I had persuaded him to this view.* It seemed then that the matter of ascription had been satisfactorily resolved.

But things are never that simple. When I returned in 1996 to a study of Sarah Grimké's papers at the Clements Library, there was a new archivist, Robin Cox. I discussed with him the problems I had in ascribing this essay and asked for his professional opinion. Again, he compared the manuscript of the essay with letters written and signed by Angelina and Sarah during the same decade. Without hesitation, he declared the manuscript to have been written by Sarah. I cite from his written statement, by permission:

> While the sisters' hands are similar in some respects, they differ strongly in the way the ampersands are formed. The ampersands in "Marriage" [replaced in this book by the word "and"] are unlike

---

* Carl Degler, *At Odds: Women and the Family in America from the Revolution to the Present* (New York: Oxford University Press, 1980), 265.

Angelina's simple "crossed" ampersands, but are identical with Sarah's distinctively looped ones. Furthermore, the general shape and orientation of the writing more closely resembles the more vertical, open hand of Sarah than Angelina's tighter, highly slanted hand.

There is nothing nicer for a scholar than having an expert confirm one's judgement. Frankly, I had never paid any attention to the formation of ampersands, which, according to Mr. Cox, were the first things one should look at in nineteenth-century handwriting. Now his letter would go with the other letters into the manuscript file and all was well.

Until the day before I was going to leave for home. That day I read an exchange of letters between Sarah Grimké and her brother Frederick, a judge in Cincinnati, Ohio, which began in 1852 when she asked him for information about the laws pertaining to divorce. Frederick Grimké was pro-slavery and had learnedly written on the subject. There was little or no contact between him and the sisters during the time of their greatest antislavery activity, but in the 1850s Sarah turned to him for information about laws pertaining to women and he answered her at length and with some objectivity. Apparently, at that time, Sarah began to send him some of her printed writings, on which he commented. In 1858, he read her essay "Rights of Woman" and requested that it should be published anonymously, which must have seemed like a rebuke to Sarah.

In his next letter, written November 23, 1858, Frederick reiterated that request and continued:

With regard to Angelina's Article on marriage I intended on my last visit to Eagle Wood to say a few words. . . . think there are passages which are too gross and [paper torn here] therefore should be altered or modified so as to express the same ideas and yet so as to be in accordance with the char[acter] and most refined feelings. Chastity and refinement of taste is nothing more or less than the triumph of the higher over the lower part of our nature. If Angelina will do as I wish her Essay will have a weight, influence, and circulation, which it will not otherwise have.*

* Letter, Frederick Grimké to Sarah Grimké, November 23, 1858, WELD MSS.

"Angelina's article on marriage . . ." Well, back to square one. Here was a primary source ascribing the article to Angelina. It takes two primary sources for a historian to assert something as a fact. Here was one, naming Angelina as the author. The stylistic evidence and the various references to the same subject matter in different letters and essays by Sarah Grimké were primary source evidence for Sarah being the author. I continued reading Frederick Grimké's letters. Many of them were missing, and only a few of her letters to him were extant.

In the summer of 1859, Frederick again referred to one of Sarah's essays, which she had submitted to him for critique. His comments were scathing:

> I received safely your communication on the right of female suffrage; but why did you select such an inferior journal to publish in. Can it be possible that there is not one in the whole East, which has a commanding character, and extensive influence. I presume, however, that you regard the pages which you have written, merely tentative, as only preparatory to a wider, and more thorough investigation. No subject of great moment, and especially if it is of great novelty, can be adequately handled, unless after great thought, and a severe discipline of the reasoning faculties. . . . *

This was followed by a lengthy disquisition on how and why the sexes are naturally different. The tone of this letter, as of his other letters, was patronizing in its unquestioned authoritative stance. Sarah had sent him an essay; he dismissed it as merely a tentative draft, without bothering to give any reason for such dismissal. If he had done this in 1859, he might have done it earlier. If so, was it possible that Sarah had hesitated to submit her essay on marriage to him under her own name and had conspired with Angelina to pass it off as Angelina's? Frederick was more respectful toward Angelina, who was a public personality and a married woman. Could it have been that the discussion of sexual matters by a woman would have appeared to Frederick Grimké less shocking if presented by a married woman, as Professor Degler had suggested? If so, might this

---

* Letter, Frederick Grimké to Sarah Grimké, July 30, 1859, WELD MSS.

be the reason for the existence of a copy in Angelina's handwriting of Sarah's essay on marriage?

This is a not implausible explanation, but, of course, it ignores the evidence of the ampersands and of the most recent handwriting ascription. Either way, some expert evidence has to be disregarded. Either way, there are some pros and cons. Professor Degler, whom I informed of this latest development, reaffirmed his belief that the author was Angelina, but he also suggested that the authorship did not, in this case, much matter. Either one of the sisters was the author and what they had to say about sexuality and marriage was significant.

As of now, I believe the essay is Sarah's. But I no longer can assert this as a proven fact. I believe this essay represents the clearest and most advanced feminist statements made by Sarah Grimké to which many of the documents in this book point the way.

❧ 12 ❧

SMG, Manuscript Essay:
Marriage

The essay "Marriage," of which the major part is here printed, offers the modern reader an unusually clear insight into the way nineteenth-century feminists linked sexuality with the subjugation of women. Sarah Grimké argued that unwanted pregnancies and economic dependence were the chief causes of women's oppression in marriage and mentioned the double standard and the existence of prostitution as intrinsically connected with these evils. In her earlier work she had presented a well-documented biblical and natural rights argument for the emancipation of women, advocating education and equal rights before the law as the chief remedies. This was similar to the Wollstonecraft argument, with which she was familiar. But Sarah Grimké had earlier shown an acute awareness of the pernicious influence of what we would today call sex role indoctrination and had vigorously stressed the need for women to build self-confidence. In the fragmentary essay "Sisters of Charity," she had strongly argued for "self-reliance" and self-definition for women. In "Marriage" she raised a demand for women's control over their own bodies, a concept which puts her in advance of feminist thinkers of her day. That she could conceptualize such a demand only in terms of voluntary chastity is a reflection of her upbringing and makes her representative of her time and place.

§⤚ §⤚ §⤚

MARRIAGE

In the summer of 1855 the *New York Times* professing to give a history of the rise and progress of what is called "Free Love" identified it with the Woman's Rights movement. This writer says, "The Woman's Rights movement leads directly and rapidly in the same direction, viz. to Free Love, that extreme section of it we mean which claims to rest upon the absolute and indefeasible right of woman to equality in all respects with man and to a complete sovereignty over her own person and conduct."

This exposition of the *principles* of the Woman's Rights movement I heartily accept. We do claim the absolute and indefeasible right of woman to an equality in all respects with man and to a complete sovereignty over her own person and conduct. Human rights are *not* based upon sex, color, capacity or condition. They are universal, inalienable and eternal, and none but despots will deny to woman that supreme sovereignty over her own person and conduct which Law concedes to man.

The conclusion that this writer draws from this equality of rights, viz., that this "movement leads directly and rapidly to the principles of 'Free Love'," or that a claim for woman's rights "nullifies the very idea of marriage as anything more than a partnership at will," I utterly deny. Man is acknowledged to have rightfully supreme sovereignty over *his own* person and conduct, and yet, who believes that this nullifies marriage, making it in *his* case a mere partnership at will? Why then should it be so in the case of woman? Is *she* less worthy of being trusted with this right than he? Let the 20,000 prostitutes of New York whose virtue is often bought by *married* men answer. Is *her* heart more inconstant and less penetrated than his by the love of children? Even if experience had not taught us otherwise, the nature of the two beings would determine the question. . . . Is it not wonderful that woman has endured so long and so patiently the hidden wrongs which man has inflicted upon her *in* the marriage relation, and all because her heart so cleaves to her children and to home and to *one* love, that she silently buries her sorrows and immolates herself rather than surrender her heart's dearest treasures.

Let us examine these assertions calmly, reverently, for we are treading upon holy ground: all *rights* are *holy*. Let us first look at the effect upon the marriage relation of the hitherto acknowledged principle that man had rights superior to woman. Has it not subordinated her to his passions? Has she not been continually forced into a motherhood which she abhorred, because she knew that her children were *not* the offspring of Love but of Lust? Has she not in unnumbered instances felt in the deepest recesses of her soul, that she was used to minister to Passion, not voluntarily to receive from her husband the chaste expression of his *love?* Has she not, too often, when thus compelled to receive the germ *she could not welcome*, refused to retain and nourish into life the babe, which she felt was not the fruit of a pure connubial love?

Ponder well the effects upon woman of the *assumed superiority of rights* in the stronger sex, that sex too in which the constitutional element of sex has far greater strength. Look too at the effect upon children, who are the product of such *one-sided rights*—puny, sickly, ill-organized and unbalanced—bearing about in body and mind the marks of their unholy origin.

And yet the Times is horror-struck at the idea of woman's claiming "*A supreme sovereignty over her own person and conduct.*" Is it not time that she should? Has not man proved himself unworthy of the power which he assumes over her person and conduct? How I ask has *he* protected and cherished her? Let her faded youth, her shatter'd constitution, her unharmonious offspring, her withered heart and *his* withered intellect answer these questions. Is it not time then that she asked for "a redress of grievances" and a recognition of that *equality of rights* which alone can save her?

Let us now look at the results of such a recognition. A right on the part of woman to decide *when* she shall become a mother, how often and under what circumstances. Surely as upon her alone devolves the necessity of nurturing unto the fulness of life the being within her and after it is born, of nursing and tending it thro' helpless infancy and capricious childhood, often under the pressure of miserable health, she *ought* to have the right of controlling all preliminaries. If man had all these burdens to bear, would not *he* declare that common sense and common justice confer this right upon him.

An eminent physician of Boston once remarked that if in the economy of nature, the sexes alternated in giving birth to children no family would ever have more than three, the husband bearing one and the wife two. But the *right* to decide this matter has been almost wholly denied to woman. How often is she forced into an untimely motherhood which compels her to wean her babe, thus depriving it of that nutriment provided by nature as the most bland and fitting, during the period of dentition. Thousands of deaths from this cause, in infancy, are attributed by superstition and ignorance to the dispensations of Divine Providence. How many thousands, too, of miscarriages are forced upon woman by the fact that man lives down that law of his being which would protect her from such terrible consequences just as animal instinct protects the female among brutes. To save woman from legalized licentiousness is then one of the reasons why we plead for *equality of rights*.

No one can fail to see that this condition of things results from several causes:

1st Ignorance of those physical laws which every man and woman *ought* to know before marriage, the knowledge of which has been withheld from the young, under a false and fatal idea of delicacy. Many a man ruins his own health and that of his wife and his children too, thro' ignorance. A diffusion of knowledge respecting these laws would greatly lessen existing evils.

2nd A false conception in man and woman of *his* nature and necessities. The great truth that the most concentrated fluid of the body has an office to perform in the production of *great tho'ts and original ideas*, as well as in the reproduction of the species is known to few and too little appreciated by all. The prodigal waste of this by legalized licentiousness has dwarfed the intellect of man. . . .

3rd The fact that many legal marriages are not love marriages. In a pure, true relation between the sexes, no difficulties can ever arise, but a willing recognition of each other's rights and mutual wants, naturally and spontaneously resulting in voluntary motherhood, a joyful appreciation of the blessedness of parentage, the birth of healthy, comely children and a beautiful home.

But it may be asked, what is to be done in cases of uncongenial marriages. Are not such men and women to follow their attractions outside of the legal relation. I unhesitatingly answer no! Where two persons have established a false marriage relation, *they are bound to abide by the consequences* of the mistake they have made. Perhaps they did love each other, but a nearer intimacy has frozen this love or changed it into disgust. Or theirs may have been a marriage of convenience or one for the sake of obtaining a house, a fortune, a position in life or it may have been a mere act of obedience to parents, or of gratitude, or a means of canceling a monied obligation. Multiform are the *unworthy* motives which seduce men and women into this sacred relation. In all these cases, let them abide the consequences of their own perversion of marriage in exchanging personal chastity for the pride of life, vanity in dress, position or a house to live in without that *love* which alone can make that house a *home*.

In some cases, it may be duty for the parties to separate, but let both keep themselves pure, so long as both are living. Let them accept the discipline thus afforded, and spiritual strength and growth will be their reward.

The Doctrine that human beings are to follow their attractions, which lies at the base of that miscalled "free love" system, is fraught with infinite danger. We are too low down to listen for one moment to its syren voice. . . .

Let me then exculpate "the woman's rights movement," from the charge of "tending directly and rapidly to the Free Love system, and nullifying the very idea of Marriage as anything more than a partnership at will." On the contrary our great desire is to purify and exalt the marriage relation and destroy *all* licentiousness. To every unhappy couple we say again, bear in quiet home seclusion, the heart withering consequences of your own mistakes. You owe this to yourselves, to your children, to society. Keep yourselves pure from that desecration of the marriage relation, which brings children into the world who have not upon their brows the seals of love and chastity. If you cannot live thus purely together and separation becomes necessary, let no temporary or permanent relation be formed by either party during the life of the other. . . .

In marriage is the origin of life. In the union of the sexes exists a creative energy which is found nowhere else. Human nature tends to the uses of all the faculties with which it is endowed, and desire is strong in proportion to the greatness of the result which flows from its exercise. Hence the creative is stronger than any other faculty, birth being the *great* fact of our existence here, and its *legitimate* exercise is the natural result of the purest and most unselfish love, the spontaneous giving away of oneself to the only loved one and the receiving of that other to ourselves in return. Marriage is a necessity of our being, because of our halfness. Every man and woman feels a profound want, which no father nor mother, no sister nor brother can fill. An indescribable longing for, and yearning after a perfect absorbing of its interests, feeling and being itself into one kindred spirit. The man feels within him a lack of the feminine element, the woman the lack of the masculine, each possessing enough of the other's nature to appreciate it and seek its fulness [sic], each in the other. Each has a deep awareness of incompleteness without the other . . . and seek[s] that divinity in her and in him, with whom they would companion for life. *This divinity* is the only true basis of union, out of it alone grow these holy affinities which bind soul to soul, not only in a temporal relation but in an eternal marriage . . .

/Wherever this strong deep affection, this indissoluble marriage of spirit with spirit, does not prompt to the union of the sexes, wherever a momentary physical excitement is all that is sought, then mutual pollution and self degradation is the consequence. In every true marriage, the husband and wife become one, by irrepressible affinities. This soul oneness finds its most natural, most scared and intense outward expression in that mutual personal embrace, which in the order of God, constitutes them Creators, exercising divine functions and ushering into being immortal existence. Some regard the termination of the childbearing period in woman as Nature's interdict upon sexual intercourse between man and woman. To me that embrace is as spontaneous an expression of love in husband and wife *after* that period as before it, and as natural and pure as the kisses press'd by the loving child upon its mothers lips, or that Mother's yearning pressure of her child to her bosom. If it be the outbirth of overflowing affection and spiritual affinity pervading each others' being with the aroma of faith in and love for the intrinsic qualities of character, then why repress this mode of manifestation which will never cease to be natural until disease or the infirmities of age have deadened all physical susceptibilities?

Married persons sometimes have no children, nor any hope of them. How then, can this fact render physical connection an inappropriate expression of *their* mutual love? For altho' the desire for children is a natural excitement to the sexual act, yet that is weak in comparison with that yearning for a mutual *absorption into each* *other*, which alone gives vitality to every true marriage, and the ceasing to have children does not and cannot destroy this deep abiding feeling. . . . /*

Full well do multitudes of human beings know in bitterness of soul, that the empty ceremony of a priest and connubial relations do *not* constitute marriage. Many a woman (I call her not *wife*) loathes the unhallowed connection she has formed and would gladly welcome death as deliverer from that polluted prison house, which the world *miscalls* her *home*. A revolting experience has forced upon her the conviction that she is a legal prostitute, a chattel personal, a tool that is used, a mere convenience—and too late does she learn that those who desecrate the marriage relation sin against their own bodies and their own souls, for no crime carries with it such physical suffering or so deep a sense of *self* degradation. . . .

Man seems to feel that Marriage gives him the control of Woman's person just as the Law gives him the control of her property. Thus are her most sacred rights destroyed by that very act, which, under the laws of Nature should enlarge, establish and protect them. In marriage is the origin of Life—in it woman finds herself endowed with a creative energy she never possessed before, in it new aspirations take possession of her, an indescribable longing after motherhood as the felt climax of her being. She joyfully gives herself away, that she may receive the germ of a new being, and true to nature, would fain retire within herself and absorb and expend all her energies in the development of this precious germ. But alas! How few are permitted unmolested to pursue that end, which for the time being, has become the great object of life. How often is she compelled by various considerations to yield to the *unnatural* embraces of her husband, and thus to endanger the very existence of her embryo babe. How often is it sacrificed to the ungoverned passion of its own father and the health of the mother seriously impaired. Every unnatural process is deleterious, hence abortions are destructive to the constitution and many women are broken down in the prime of life by them alone, and their haggard countenances too plainly reveal their secret sorrows. A lady once said to me I have but one child, but I have had 12 miscarriages—another had 4 children and 15

---

* The preceding two-paragraph section, set off by slashes, has been moved forward from its place in the manuscript.

abortions. And why I would ask this untimely casting of her fruit? Do the beasts of the field miscarry? Why not? *They* are governed by instinct. Are the *brutes* safe during the period of gestation whilst *woman* is not?

. . . Again—look at the burdens imposed upon her by the care of many children following in quick succession. How can any mother do her duty to her family, if in 8 years she have 6 children. Look at the unnatural tax upon her constitution, her night watches, her sore vexations and trials and causes nameless and numberless that wear away her life. If men had to alternate with their wives, the duties of the nursery, fewer and further between would be its inmates . . .

O! how many women who have entered the marriage relation in all purity and innocence, expecting to realize in it the completion of their own halfness, the rounding out of their own being, the blending of their holiest instincts with those of a kindred spirit, have too soon discovered that they were unpaid housekeepers and nurses, and still worse, chattels personal to be used and abused at the will of a master, and all in a cold matter of course way. O! the agony of realizing that personal and pecuniary independence are annihilated by that "Law which makes the husband and wife *one* and that one is the husband." How many so called wives, rise in the morning oppressed with a sense of degradation from the fact that their chastity has been violated, their holiest instincts disregarded, and themselves humbled under an oppressive sense of their own pollution, and that, too, a thousand times harder to bear, because so called husband has been the perpetrator of the unnatural crime. . . .

Who does not see that Men must grow out of that nondevelopment in which they now are, before they will have ears to hear or hearts to love the truth on this subject, and that to Woman must be conceded an *equality of rights* thro'out the circle of human relations, before she can be emancipated from that worst of all slaveries—slavery to the passions of Man.

And this equality cannot—will not be conceded until she too grows out of that stratum of development in which she now is. Her imperfect education unfits her for acquiring that pecuniary independence which would lift her above the temptation to marry for a home. Dependence subjects her too often to be duped *in* the marriage relation as well as out of it. And the great work to be done now for woman by woman, is to impress her with the necessity of pecuniary independence, each working out that independence according to her taste and ability. Now they work under great disadvantages and can obtain a mere pittance. But be not discouraged sisters—Is not a dinner of herbs and simple apparel such as you can provide infinitely better than sumptuous fare, costly attire, elegant furniture and equipage received in exchange for *freedom and personal purity.* They must yearn to be *women* rather than fine statues to be draped in satins and lawns—elegant automatons grac[ing] a drawing room, or pretty play things to be toyed with by respectable rakes or heartless dandies under the guise of lovers and husbands. . . .

In all great changes thro' which Society passes in her upward progress, there seem to be periods of interregnum, when the old usage has died out before the new one was ready to be inaugurated in its place. . . .

Let the old contract system remain, until that new and divine form of spirit union, shall have gently undermined its hold upon society, pushing it gradually off & taking its place in the hearts and lives of all who are prepared to welcome it in purity and love . . .

❧ 13 ❧

SMG to Jeanne Deroin

Jeanne Deroin (1810?–1894), a seamstress, was a leader of St. Simonian women in France. Together with Pauline Roland she organized working-class women and was editor of a women's newspaper during the 1830 revolution. After its collapse she continued to advocate feminist socialism. Married in 1832, she refused to take her husband's name. Still active in the revolution of 1848, she and others formed a new women's club and issued a paper, *Women's Voices (Voix des Femmes)*. The paper was quickly closed down by the new government, workers' organizations were outlawed and women were forbidden membership in political clubs. Jeanne Deroin promptly announced her candidacy for the next assembly election in 1849. During her campaign, she declared that a government made up of men was incapable of representing the entire population. She was defeated.

She and Roland then organized women's cooperatives and were elected members of the Central Committee of Associative Unions [cooperatives of working people]. In 1850 both were arrested for conducting political movements and received six months in jail. After her release from jail, Deroin left France and lived in exile.*

* Bonnie S. Anderson and Judith P. Zinsser, *A History of Their Own: Women in Europe from Prehistory to the Present*, 2 vols. (New York: Har-

116

Sarah Grimké most likely knew about Jeanne Deroin through a letter she and Pauline Roland wrote from jail to US women assembled at the 1851 Worcester Woman's Rights Convention. Excerpts from the letter follow:

To the Convention of Women in America:
. . . The Assembly [of the revolutionary government of 1848] kept silence in regard to the right of one-half of humanity. . . .
No mention was made of woman in a Constitution framed in the name of Liberty, Equality, and Fraternity. . . . But while those selected by half the people—by men alone—evoke force to stifle liberty, and forge restrictive laws to establish order by compression, woman, guided by fraternity . . . makes an appeal to the laborer to found liberty and equality on fraternal solidarity. . . . The delegates of a hundred and four associations, united, without distinction of sex, elected two women, with several of their brethren, to participate equally with them in the administration of the interest of labor, and in the organization of the work of solidarity. . . . It is in the name of law framed by man only—by those elected by privilege—that the Old World . . . has shut up within the walls of a prison . . . those elected by the laborers. But the impulse has been given, a grand act has been accomplished. The right of woman has been recognized by the laborers. . . .
Sisters of America! your socialist sisters of France are united with you in the vindication of the right of woman to civil and political equality. We have . . . the profound conviction that only by the power of association based on solidarity—by the union of the working-classes of both sexes to organize labor—can be acquired, completely and pacifically, the civil and political equality of woman, and the social right for all. . . . Jeanne Deroin, Pauline Roland.*

Apparently, judging from the opening of Sarah's letter, she had in 1855 or '56 come across some of the "almanacs" Deroin published from her exile in Britain. She makes no reference whatever to Deroin's revolutionary past, her suffering in prison and exile, her socialist-feminist ideas. Instead, she responds to Deroin's sense of solidarity

per & Row, 1988), II; 377–78, 381, and Bonnie G. Smith, *Changing Lives: Women in European History Since 1700* (Lexington, Mass.: D. C. Heath & Co.,1989), 241–42.

* Elizabeth Cady Stanton, Susan B. Anthony and Matilda Joselyn Gage (eds.), *History of Woman Suffrage: 1848–1861*, 2 vols. (New York: Fowler and Wells, 1881, I:234–37.

with the men of her class, the "laborers," and states her own view of the relations of the sexes. It is a much different view than she had expressed in *Letters on the Equality of the Sexes* and in her more recent essay "Marriage." Obviously influenced by popularized evolutionary ideas, she traces a story of "progress," in which men and women developed out of savagery into the enlightened nineteenth century state of civilization. She seems to exonerate men from any responsibility in the past of oppressing women. "Woman has been in all ages the recipient, man the giver. He has been the guardian, she the guarded." This is an astonishing statement, coming from her. But in the succeeding paragraphs Sarah reverts to her usual stance of describing women as agents for progress and for the common good. "Another phase of humanity is now before us. . . . [M]an has trampled in the dust . . . the rights of his fellow-man, . . . [he] has swallowed up in his love of supremacy the sacred distinction between matter and mind, and [over] whelmed all in one common ruin, to render mankind subservient to his will." The juxtaposition of these two seemingly contradictory statements about man's role can be explained by Sarah's then current belief in a divinely ordained evolution. The "savage" and martial state of mind of man in the past was part of God's design, but it has lasted too long; it has outlived its usefulness. Now it is woman's turn "in the race to Progress, to Liberty, to Equality."

Sarah describes woman's emancipatory mission in religious terms. Woman is God's "still small voice"; refined through suffering, she will accomplish her great mission of redeeming the world in love, united with "redeemed" men.

In the last paragraph of this letter Sarah Grimké writes about woman: "The world can never know, except through inference, the dangers and the darkness of the past she has trodden, but the discipline has not been lost upon her. It was exactly what she needed to prepare her . . ." One might substitute the word "I" for "she" to gain a better understanding of the psychological state of the author. In several of her personal letters during these years Sarah had used similar phrases to describe her state of mind. Her ambition had been crushed, her high hopes for accomplishment had been smashed; ultimately, what would help her to stay on an even keel and persist in a positive stance toward life, was her religion.

ༀ ༀ ༀ

LETTER TO JEANNE DEROIN
EDITOR OF "WOMEN'S ALMANAC," PUBLISHED IN LONDON

Eagleswood School, May 21, 1856.

Dear Friend:

... Your almanacs for 1853 and '54 have recently fallen into my hands, and I have greatly enjoyed the perusal of them. I fear, like almost all our efforts to sustain a periodical devoted to the elevation of woman, that has failed to receive the support necessary to maintain it. One reason doubtless is, that the men hold the pursestrings, and rightly so, since by their labor chiefly the purses are filled; but principally because of the little interest felt by women in this great reform. If women were prepared to prosecute this enterprise in a noble, generous, self-sacrificing spirit, there would be no difficulty; but that they are not is too sorrowfully true to admit of a doubt. ... It is manifest that our present task is to arouse our own sex to a sense of their debased condition, to a willingness to shake off the chains of sloth and self-indulgence, to wake to their fearful responsibilities, and offer themselves a willing sacrifice on the altar of Human Rights. ...

Hitherto, woman has seemed to expect, that the repeal of onerous and disgraceful laws will instantly, as by magic, prepare her to enter on new fields of usefulness and duty. So thinking, she doth greatly err. The repeal of every unrighteous statute cannot do for her the inner work which must be done, ere she is to move the lever which will elevate humanity. I do not mean that she is not to labor for the revocation of partial and unjust laws; but while intent on this object, let her see to it that she is preparing herself to aid in the enactment of such as will be a blessing to the whole world. Let her *patiently and wisely study the past,* she will see that she has no cause of complaint against her brethren; that she, as well as they, have worked out the problem of life according to the development of each; that men have done for us in by-gone ages what seemed best and wisest for the general welfare. The lower elements of our nature being more largely developed in men, they were greatly our superiors in physical strength; and as every thing finds its level, we naturally fell into that subordinate station which best suited our capabilities of action. This epoch was the reign of animal power, but the exercise of this power unfolded the intellect, because the various means necessary to compass certain ends improved and strengthened the thinking faculty, called forth ingenuity, set in motion, more or less, all the powers of the mind. Hence we find man in the field of intellect, as in the camp and in the court, the superior of woman, the arbiter of her fate, the framer of the laws by which she was governed, and justly so, because in those points first in the order of human development, man had arrived much nearer the fulness [sic] of strength than woman, who was yet in her infancy, or in the immaturity of youth. During these stages of human progress, man, notwithstanding the almost excrescent growth of his animal propensities, exercised a kindly care, a fraternal solicitude, to spare woman from those hardships, both physical and mental, which he had to endure. Woman has been in all ages the recipient, man the giver. He has been the guardian, she the guarded. . . .

Another phase of humanity is now before us. Woman, who has been hidden from the public eye, is now summoned to the theatre of action. Let her go forth and stand upon the mount before the Lord. She will see the meaning of what the prophet saw—"A great and strong wind passed by, and brake the mountain, and rent the rock in pieces, but the Lord was not in the wind; and after the wind an earthquake, but the Lord was not in the earthquake; and after the earthquake a fire, and after the fire, a still small voice." Man has exhibited on the arenas of life the wind, the earthquake, and the fire. He has let loose his stormy passions, he has trampled in the dust and ground to powder with the hoofs of his battle-horse the rights of his fellow-man, he has caused the mightiest kingdoms to quail before the breath of his nostrils, to quiver like a reed shaken by the wind; he has swallowed up in his love of supremacy the sacred distinction between matter and mind, and whelmed all in one common ruin, to render mankind subservient to his will. Has man, then, tyrannized over woman more than he has tyrannized over man? Let the army of martyrs answer. Let the thunders of a Luther's voice, the dying agonies of Jerome of Prague and John Huss [sic] and [a] million others, who testified against the usurpation of tyrants, answer the query. The response will come, like deep answering to deep, reverberating from age to age, proclaiming that man has oppressed man with as much, nay, more severity, than he has oppressed woman. And here let me ask if woman has not been but too faithful a copyist of man, and exercised, in her narrow sphere, an authority as arbitrary and imperious as man?

Let us, then, not blame the past,—a past ordained by the changeless laws of God,—a past which was necessary to the glorious future. . . . If woman would do her work in the most perfect manner, she must be the still small voice of God. She can gain no moral victory, except she be endowed with "power from on high." To prepare her for her mission, what infinite pains has Jehovah taken! He has hid her in the hollow of his hand from the devastating effects of military glory; he has shielded her from the corrupting influence of irresponsible power; he has saved her from the arduous, wearing, health-destroying intellectual efforts which man has been compelled to make in the toilsome and difficult task of elaborating mind. He has been her forerunner—the John Baptist of humanity. She is now reaping material and intellectual fields she did not sow, and enjoying a rich harvest from those labors she did not participate. Gratefully, most gratefully, do I recognise the ceaseless labors of man. Thankfully do I partake of the fruits he has cultivated. In rendering him honor, I feel that I render it where honor is due.

But man has now arrived at a crisis where his prowess as a warrior is nearly useless, when the attainments of intellect, however grand, the discoveries of science, however important, do not fill up the wants of his being, and he longs unspeakably, irrepressibly, for the development of that higher, holier element of his being, his rational or spiritual nature. . . . If man has been thus gradually ascending in the scale of being, if the untutored savage has been transformed into the civilized man, if the warrior has sheathed his sword in accordance with the demands of his nobler nature, if the war ship has been changed into the merchant vessel, if all betokens progress, and the watchword of the advanced guard of humanity is "Excelsior," has not woman shared in the general improvement? Has she not risen in intelligence and virtue? Is not her conception of "woman as she should be" broadened, deepened and elevated? Is there not in her heart a responsive thrill to the voice which is calling the race to Progress, to Liberty, to Equality? Who can doubt it? The same divine hand which so long shrouded her in the secret of Jehovah's pavilion, has sustained her through every refining process, and although the furnace has ofttimes [*sic*] been heated seven times hotter, God has ever been near to save the pure gold. And now that He begins to see His own image reflected in the molten metal, He rejoices, and is preparing to take it from the crucible, and coin and stamp and circulate it through the social mass.

The sufferings of woman, her trials, her baptism, are . . . exactly what she needed to prepare her to usher in the day when LOVE will reign; when woman, having none but righteous ends to gain, will not stoop to artifice and circumvention, but will accomplish her purpose by philosophy and religion. Let her, then, labor, courageously, incessantly, hopefully, to redeem herself, that she may be worthy to aid in redeeming her brethren. Hitherto, the history of man has been written in blood,

> Spotted o'er with human blood,
> And big with crime and strife.

The history of woman has been written in tears. May their future united history be radiant with deeds of benevolence, LOVE and UNITY!

SARAH M. GRIMKÉ

ﭑ 14 ﭑ

SMG to Gerrit Smith

In 1851 the daughter of the wealthy New York reformer Gerrit Smith visited her friend Amelia Bloomer and her father's cousin, Elizabeth Cady Stanton, in the village of Seneca Falls, N.Y. She had been raised according to the reformist principles of her father, given the same education as a boy and encouraged by him to wear loose, comfortable clothing. Now she appeared in a costume she herself had designed, a short tunic worn over "Turkish trousers." The dress impressed her friend Amelia Bloomer, who wrote about it in her feminist paper, *The Lily,* and shortly after adopted it, as did about fifteen other women, among them Elizabeth Cady Stanton and the Grimké sisters. A picture of the costume, which would enter history as "the Bloomer costume," appeared in the July 1851 issue of the paper. All during that year various correspondents, among them Elizabeth Cady Stanton, wrote in favor of women adopting this costume.

The public's dismay at the Bloomer costume and the ridicule heaped upon it in the press helped to spread it and the idea of dress reform. The circu-lation of *The Lily* increased sharply and various correspondents widened the debate to include the issues of women's autonomy and women's health. Many of the male reformers adopted a tolerantly neutral stance, while some of the husbands and sons of women who wore it became embarrassed by the negative response of the general public.

Late in December 1855 Gerritt Smith wrote a letter to his cousin, Elizabeth Cady Stanton, in which he expressed the opinion that the woman's rights movement was "not in the proper hands and the proper hands are not yet to be found." He considered all woman's rights conventions "failures." What was wrong with the leaders of the movement, according to Smith, was that they dressed conventionally in dresses that imprisoned and crippled them by stressing their help-lessness, their inability to work to support themselves and their desire to please men. While he conceded that dress was "not the primal cause of [women's] helplessness and degradation," it still was a sym-bol of the false doctrines which degraded women. He urged women to fight against old habits and false ideas about women's "delicacy" and to adopt a simple costume. He predicted that once dress reform was adopted "an easy victory will follow."*

Elizabeth Cady Stanton answered her cousin in a friendly tone but refused to concede any of his points. First of all, she reminded him that only women could know what it feels like to be a woman. She regarded the woman's rights movement not as a failure but thought that women in the majority had developed to the point of discontent, a condition which, among men, had been enough to bring on the American Revolution. "The steps between discontent and action are few and short indeed." She deplored women's restricted education but cited as the worst evil the fate of drunkards' wives kept in deg-radation by marriage. Woman, she asserted, feels her deepest wrongs, her silent agony in "those sacred relations of which we speak not in our conventions." It was a question "of human rights—the sacred right of woman to her own person, to all her God-given powers of body and soul. . . . Here," she stated,

is the starting-point; here is the battleground where our independence must be fought and won. A true marriage relation has far more to do with the elevation of woman than the style and cut of her dress. Dress is . . . changeable, transient . . . but institutions, supported by laws, can be overturned but by revolution.*

* Anthony Stanton, et al., *History of Woman Suffrage*, I:836–39; quotes, 836, 837, 839.
* *Ibid.* Stanton's letter, 839–42; short quotes, 840; long quote, 841.

Stanton would not defend womens' current dress, but thought that if dress reform was to be made, woman should dress like men.

This debate, which Stanton considered important enough to include in the first volume of her *History of Woman Suffrage*, explains the charged meanings of dress reform. The fifteen or more women who adopted the Bloomer costume in 1852 did so for practical and symbolic reasons. They were active women, some of them working women, others public speakers and itinerant lecturers, and the ease of wearing pants and a short overskirt rather than crinolines, bustles, whalebone corsets and many petticoats made their daily lives considerably more comfortable. By wearing the costume in public they made a symbolic statement about "the new woman" and used the issue of dress reform to spread their ideas on woman's rights and wrongs. The publicity and public attacks they and their families had to suffer as a result of wearing the Bloomer costume caused most of them to abandon the practice rather quickly. The above exchange of letters was undoubtedly an effort on the part of reformers to bolster the courage of the dress reformers and convince them to persist in wearing the "Turkish costume."

Gerrit Smith was given to sudden enthusiasms and quick judgments. Like many male reformers he did not doubt the propriety of advising women what were the main issues for their emancipation movement. Stanton rejected his patronizing attitude and informed him what *women* thought the main issues were. It is very interesting to note that this early in the campaign for woman's rights Stanton already considered "the right to her person" a key issue. Later interpretations have stressed Stanton's emphasis on the ballot at the Seneca Falls convention, but here she chose to focus on what today we would call a "woman's right to her own body" as the central issue for women.

Several other women responded with much sharper criticism than had Stanton to Gerrit Smith's position. In August 1856 Sarah Grimké weighed in with a letter to Gerrit Smith, which was in October printed in *The Lily*. She disagreed sharply with his negative assessment of the leadership of the woman's rights movement. Reviewing, as she had in previous essays and letters, the past history of woman as "the plaything of man, a being created for him . . . to minister to his material comfort, to surrender herself to the gratification of his passions and appetites," she found that woman had now reached a new level of maturity. She again presented her evolutionary argument and traced the progress women had made. "I cannot but believe that her cause is in the right hands. She must do the work of elevation herself. No power out of herself can do it for her," she argued. She rejected Smith's assertion that the sexes must of necessity be assigned to different spheres of activity. "Although I assert an essential difference between the sexes," she stated, "I admit that they have a common nature, physically, intellectually, and spiritually." Reviewing once again her arguments for the moral superiority of women, she looked toward a future marked by "the elevation of woman, and the spiritual advancement of man."

It is interesting to note that Angelina Grimké, who had confined her literary productions in the years 1840–57 to brief resolutions or letters to the various woman's rights conventions, produced a lengthy article on "Dress Reform" in 1857 which was published in *The Daily Standard* on June 10, 1857. The article is based in its entirety on Sarah's arguments. Angelina elaborated and contextualized these arguments by presenting them in a historical framework, a sort of simple women's history, tracing "progress." The conceptual framework is so similar to Sarah's, as she expressed it in the various articles and essays discussed in this volume, that one might conclude the article in the Standard was a joint product of the sisters. But it was not; Sarah, in one of her letters, refers to Angelina's working hard on a long essay on dress reform. One novel contribution made by Angelina is her linking of the dress issue with that of work:

> If woman means to *work,* let her dress herself for *work.* . . . [Man] *never can accept her as a helper meet* for such work, while she is tripping at every upward step, or must loosen her hold upon the car [of progress] in order to catch up her robe, and clear her feet of its incumbrance. . . .
>
> We are now laying the foundation of women's rights, let us dress then as workers, who have not *earned* enough yet to buy costly attire. . . . [W]hen she has educated herself into lucrative and useful occupations, *then* may she fitly expend upon her person *her own earnings,* not man's.*

* Angelina Grimké's article, WELD MSS.

ৡ৯ৡ৯ৡ৯

Eagleswood School, August 4, [1856]

Dear Gerrit. . . .*

I must confess the reform dress offends my taste; but its manifest fitness for walking in the country, through bushes and brakes, jumping fences, working in the garden, and all sorts of domestic labor, is an appeal to my common sense which I cannot resist. I therefore wear it for all such purposes, but I see no reason why it should be worn when seated quietly at home, or passing about a city, any more than a farmer who is visiting his friends or spending a few days in New York should wear his working clothes or appear in the parlor in his shirt sleeves. Appropriateness ought to govern dress, and the moderately long dress appears to me most appropriate in the city, except when engaging in domestic business, or when the walking is wet. . . .

Now, it is perfectly clear to me that the position, relations, duties, circumstances, avocations of woman do not demand such a dress at all times—that she could only wear it constantly at the sacrifice of feeling, delicacy, and convenience. Here and there you may find a Helen Weber or a Captain Betsy Smith.** If they have chosen professions which could render any womanly dress incommodious and improper, I have nothing to say. Let them follow out the proclivities of their peculiar natures; but I cannot believe that those professions, or many others, such as house and ship building, and all the rougher or more laborious occupations belong to woman, or that she will ever follow them to any extent.

True there are many kinds of business that both sexes may engage in; many of the handicraft trades are of this description, and I rejoice that women are gradually introducing themselves into employments from which they have hitherto been excluded, such as the offices of

* Sarah M. Grimké to Gerrit Smith, *The Lily*, Vol. VIII, No. 19, October 1, 1856, pp. 130–31.

** Helen Weber, a European woman who habitually wore male dress, wrote a letter to the Woman's Rights Convention at Worcester, Mass., 1851, to explain this practice. She explained that she adopted male attire as a "measure of convenience" in her business.

I have been unable to find a reference to Capt. Betsy Smith in the Proceedings of the early Woman's Rights Conventions.

clerk, salesman, bookkeeper, etc. This more extensive range of business relations, of contact with men, will operate most favorably; it cannot but produce a wider scope for thought, a greater opportunity for intellectual activity, a larger circumference of action, sharpen the powers of invention, increase the desire for usefulness and independence, and enable woman to take more comprehensive views of everything respecting herself. . . . But enough of this. The next generation will produce women of higher organization, of finer intellectual and moral development; they will not worship at the shrine of fashion, or allow themselves to be cheated of their common sense, their health, their convenience. . . .

Meanwhile, although the present laborers in the cause of human rights may fall far short of the ideal of Reformers, yet let us heartily accord to them both gratitude and praise. They have done a mighty work. . . .

I entirely dissent, my dear friend, from your affirmation, that the "Woman's Rights Movement is not in the right hands." Surely you must admit that many of the noblest, most independent, most morally exalted, most highly cultivated, most comprehensive minds are engaged in this reform. . . .

Now the past history of woman clearly proves that she has been regarded as the slave, or the plaything of man, a being *created for him*, created mainly to minister to his material comfort, to surrender herself to the gratification of his passions and appetites—at one time the object of his silly adoration, at another the machine which moved at his bidding, run [ran] in his grooves, and worked for his advantage—not exclusively, to be sure, for God has so arranged social and domestic life that whatever we do for the happiness and welfare of others always contributes to our own. Since the creation of woman, this has been her experience, her education, her discipline. Could she be other than she is? What was there in her pupilage to develop her intellect, to train her mind, to excite her to independence in thought or in action? But it was not the opinion of man respecting woman, not his treatment of her that most powerfully tended to render her imbecile, contriving, dependent, effeminate, willing to live on *his* earnings, and recline in his bowers. The debasement was infinitely more the result of her accepting his opinions as Truth, and thus losing her self-respect. But could she in her then stage of development do otherwise? Surely not; she naturally regarded him as her superior, loved her ease, hugged her chains, nor asked for a better state. But the time has come when physical forces and intellectual acumen have wrought until they are weary. Man begins to perceive that he possesses a spiritual nature of which he had hardly been cognizant, which demands nutriment of another kind, enjoyments of a higher order, incitements and exercise of a superior quality. . . .

Do we wonder that he turns to her [woman] to find spiritually what he had found materially? Shall he turn in vain? The holiest instincts of her nature answers no.

Man, in acknowledging the superiority of woman's religious nature, her greater attainments in the inner life gives her the highest assurance of his co-operation in her attempt to rise from her present degradation. He feels that there is something above power and science necessary to satisfy the yearnings of his immortal soul, and that woman is the medium through which he may receive it. She asks but time and patience—can we deny them to her?

When we remember what the condition of woman has been, how all her educational discipline has been calculated to check her aspirations after intellectual development, how she has been shut from those pursuits which render man intelligent, comprehensive, far seeing, wise to plan, strong to execute and willing to endure toil to secure independence, we may well marvel that there is as much left out of which to realize "Woman as she will be." Her "tendency to improvement must be highly spontaneous and irresistible, to have enabled her to persevere, notwithstanding the enormous faults which have at all time absorbed or neutralized" her life forces. The fact that she has been no more deteriorated by all the appliances to her lower nature, by all the drawbacks to her higher, inspires not merely a hope, but a faith that she will yet be the savior of the world in conjunction with man, under the guidance and inspiration of their common Father.

Thus regarding woman, I cannot but believe that her cause is in the right hands. She must do the work of elevation herself. No power out of herself can do it for her. . . . Let us not forget that as an intellectual being she is in her childhood or adolescence. Let us accept her for what she is, for what she must inevitably be from habit, surroundings and education, until she learns by experience what kind of woman the age calls for, and bends her powers to become what is needed. I have no fears for the success of this divinely inspired reform. My confidence in the moral endowments of my sex, and in their love of humanity is unbounded. I know they are capable of great self-sacrifice, of noble deeds, of intense suffering. I know that for this cause they have endured reproach, contumely, scorn, derision—they will endure more, and they will conquer. . . .

She is now receiving an education, passing through a discipline which she needs, and which she can only gain by a severe experience. She is acquiring knowledge which will make her see the necessity of thinking and acting for herself, undergoing an ordeal which will teach her to prize self-reliance, gaining an independence which will teach her to pursue some occupation that will secure a maintenance to herself, and enable her to aid in the support of her family. There are multitudes of women whose energies are frittered away in the little occupations of domestic life, who might and would do all they now do and turn the residue of their time to useful account, if they had some employment which was remunerative. The time, I trust is not far distant when it will be regarded as humiliating to be dependent on a father, husband, brother, cousin, etc., unless circumstances absolutely disqualify a woman for earning her own living. Custom has rendered dependence so common that it really *seems* right; but men are beginning to weary of this double burden. . . .

I cannot but hope that this appeal to the heart of woman will operate to rouse her to a sense of her obligations to do what she can towards supplying her own material wants, and this will unquestionably open to her the means of ministering to those of her intellectual nature. When she enters the path of usefulness and duty, she cannot but see the incompatibility of her present dress with true womanly dignity. I look with certainty for the time when her gewgaws and fashions will drop off as did the sword of William Penn, so soon as he was internally prepared to part with it.

You lay down another proposition, my dear friend, which I think is wholly untenable, viz. the identity of man and woman. If they are essentially the same, whence comes the difference between them? Why has man, in all ages, and in all nations, exhibited more physical strength, more intellectual power, more mental endurance, more continuity of thought, more comprehensiveness, more concentration, more invention, etc., than woman? Why has she, too, her peculiarities as strongly marked as man? She has more vivacity, more sparkle, more cheerfulness, more elasticity, more quickness of apprehension, more disinterestedness, a keener sense of justice, a greater intensity of love, a higher appreciation of spiritual things.— Difference, however, does not necessarily imply superiority in either. Each has improved the faculties bestowed, and the sexes are admirably adapted to draw out and educate the distinctive characteristics of each. It seems to me that we disparage God's work by supposing that he has created two beings identically the same, instead of giving to each particular qualities, whereby they might instruct and benefit each other. But although I assert an essential difference between the sexes, I admit they have a common nature, physically, intellectually, and spiritually. . . .

But whilst I accord to man superiority in physical strength, in all the more hardy and severe departments of the understanding, I must believe that the spiritual nature has been more highly developed in woman than in man, because it is universally conceded that the strength of the moral world lies in woman—that in her heart religion has found its home. . . .

Now it is neither physical strength nor mighty intellect that will regenerate the world. It is the unfolding of our rational nature which will introduce the spirit of gentleness, forbearance, and love and render mankind a holy brotherhood. . . . "Neither is the man without the woman, neither the woman without the man." The present conflict manifests the tendency of humanity towards a new social system—indefinite enough, but radically different from the old. This may be the negative era of social progress, but it is indispensable as a preparation for the advent of that change which will result in the elevation of woman, and the spiritual advancement of man.

Yours, most truly,
Sarah M. Grimké

❧ 15 ❧

SMG, Manuscript Essay:
Sisters of Charity

In the document below, Sarah Grimké accepts the traditional argument that women, once given equal rights, will elevate society by their gentleness and nurturing qualities but repeatedly argues that women have an inherent right to self-determination. She decries that women were deprived of rights and opportunities by law and custom and that they were made ignorant of their own power. "Woman has struggled through life with bandaged eyes, accepting the dogma of her weakness"; she has "eaten the bitter fruits of slavery." But she now seeks "to give to her whole being the opportunity to expand to its essential nobility." Sarah Grimké's ringing call for women's "self-reliance" repeats the theme of women's autonomy, which she, the first of the U.S. feminists, stressed in her other writings.

The following paragraph first appeared in the journal *SIGNS* in 1975.*

The manuscript "Sisters of Charity" consists of clippings from sources Sarah Grimké did not name, interspersed with her commentary. Undoubtedly, had she lived to carry out her project, editing and

---

* Gerda Lerner (ed. and with Intro. by), "Sarah M. Grimké's 'Sisters of Charity,' " *SIGNS: Journal of Women in Culture and Society*, vol. 1, no. 1 (Autumn 1975): 246–56. Quote, 248.

rewriting would have made the narrative more succinct. As it stands, it deserves to be studied by modern readers, not only for its content, the newness and boldness of some of its ideas, but also as a document defining the difficulties and frustrations of women intellectuals in the early nineteenth century. The powers of mind had never been allowed expansion. The education denied her, the inevitable burdens of service to other imposed on her by her upbringing and indoctrination, the sense of isolation and the loneliness imposed on her by the years of pioneering—all these speak out from the fragment before us.

The following comments first appeared in *SIGNS* in 1985.*

In the Archives section of its first issue, *SIGNS* published a document entitled "Sisters of Charity," which I edited and introduced, from the notebooks of Sarah Grimké. . . . I had read the document in the William L. Clements Library at Ann Arbor, Michigan, in 1963, as part of the Theodore Dwight Weld Manuscripts, which were at that time essentially in the state in which they had been acquired—unsorted, without chronology or annotations. Women's history as a field of inquiry and specialization did not yet exist, and I had no way of knowing the source of the clippings Grimké interspersed with her ideas and comments in her school notebook. It was quite by accident that twenty years later, when I served as a second reader for the dissertation of Diane Worzala at the University of Wisconsin–Madison, I noticed her reference to the work of nineteenth-century British feminist writer Anna Jameson.[1] The book's title, *Sisters of Charity*, struck a chord in my memory, and I asked Worzala whether by any chance the work might have been known to Grimké. Worzala kindly compared her notes and the book, *Sisters of Charity*, to my *SIGNS* reprint and was able to identify most of the quoted passages in Grimké's essay as deriving from the Jameson book.[2]

The discovery is meaningful for a number of reasons. It certainly is evidence of the intellectual interchange between American and English feminism as early as the 1850s; it also illustrates the inspiration

* These comments first appeared under the title "Comments on Lerner's 'Sarah M. Grimké's "Sisters of Charity" ' " in *SIGNS: Journal of Women in Culture and Society*, vol. 10, no. 4 (Chicago: University of Chicago Press, 1985), 811–15. This version is slightly altered and is reprinted with permission.

American women derived from the exploits and achievements of Florence Nightingale. What seems most intriguing to me is that part of her essay in which Grimké departs from and elaborates on Jameson's argument. Here we can see the strong impact of the beliefs and values derived from the American Revolution and the thoroughly radical cast of Grimké's thought.

Jameson vigorously attacks laws that disadvantage and discriminate against women, and Grimké cites Jameson in order to build a strong argument for enlarging "woman's sphere." She adds to these citations reports of Florence Nightingale's experiences in the Crimean War and in nursing the wounded. Using these clippings, Grimké argues for equal opportunities for women in professional life. "Why should idle prejudice any longer shut out women from taking their place wherever intellect rather than strength is required?" she asks (p. 142). Jameson had argued for the complementarity of the sexes because "without union of labor between the sexes nothing can be well done, because there is nothing done which does not affect the interests of both."[3] Grimké agreed wholeheartedly, but she expanded the argument. She was concerned not only with actual discrimination and the exclusion of women from economic and political participation but also with women's psychological deprivation and their lack of feminist consciousness: "At present women are depressed by the laws, depressed by a public opinion resulting from the laws, depressed by the prejudice of parents and guardians, till the great part of the sex is ignorant of its powers" (p. 142).[4]

Grimké charges that "the laws respecting married women are one of the greatest outrages that has been perpetrated against God and humanity" and that they foster "on the one side . . . injustice and oppression and on the other . . . loss of self-respect, independence and degradation" (p. 142).[5] She demands that woman be taught "self-respect and self-reliance by giving her just and equal laws" (p. 143). Grimké's impassioned outcry, often written in biblical language, goes far beyond Jameson's moderate, liberal reforms. Grimké expresses both anguish and anger and sees the antagonists as separate "classes":

> It is self evident that inequality of Rights creates antagonism and the assumption that we must continue in this state is productive of nothing but evil, because the privileged and the oppressed stand in opposition

to each other, the latter yielding unwillingly the distinctions which the former demand and the former shutting themselves up in the self made circle of their superiority and scorning even to examine the claims of the dependant class. How shall these two classes harmonize? [p. 144]

This sharply polarized vision of the relations of the sexes had been reflected in the earlier "Declaration of Sentiments" of the 1848 Seneca Falls Convention and in the more self-consciously feminist set of resolutions passed at the 1850 Ohio Woman's Rights Convention. Grimké undoubtedly had read these and may have been influenced by them. But the strong emphasis throughout her notes on the need to develop woman's feminist consciousness is her own. Elsewhere in the notes she approvingly cites an unknown source as follows: "Man never can legislate justly for woman because 'he has never entered the world to which she belongs' " (p. 144). The concept of separate "woman's culture" has seldom been expressed more forcefully. And Grimké reflects the stages of her own developing self-awareness and her hard-won sense of autonomy, which she calls the "sense of her own selfhood," in these generalizations:

> Thus far woman has struggled through life with bandaged eyes, accepting the dogma of her weakness and inability to take care of herself not only physically but intellectually. [S]he has held out a trembling hand and received gratefully the proffered aid. She has foregone her right to study the laws and purposes of the government to which she is subject. But now there is awakened in her a consciousness that she is defrauded of her legitimate Rights and that she never can fulfill [*sic*] her mission until she is placed in that position to which she feels herself called by the divinity within. [H]itherto she has surrendered her person and her individuality to man, but she can no longer do this and not feel that she is outraging her nature and her God. There is now predominant in the minds of intelligent woman to an extent never known before a struggling after freedom, an intense desire after a higher life. . . . [S]elf reliance only can create true and exalted women. [pp. 144, 146]

These ideas, to which Elizabeth Cady Stanton would later give expression and wider currency in her celebrated "Solitude of Self" lecture, reflected Sarah Grimké's spiritual crisis and emancipation from the guidance of her former mentor, Theodore Weld, and of her sister Angelina. A woman then in her sixties, Sarah Grimké had left the Weld-Grimké household in order to try to live alone and develop her latent talents. Her efforts to train for a legal or medical career failed, and she finally returned to her sister's household, where she lived the rest of her life. It is characteristic of Sarah Grimké's lifelong preoccupation with a feminist critique of Christian thought that she sees the ultimate justification of woman's striving for emancipation in her "divinity within." Over and over in her writings, Grimké asserted the equality of souls before God, the concept that "in Christ there is neither male nor female." This concept was directly opposed to centuries of biblical argument that denied women direct access to the divine and bid them to see in men (fathers, husbands, and priests) their mediators to God.

Grimké departs in yet another important way from Jameson's text and philosophical stance. The remedies she sees for the evils of gender polarization are, in her words, simple: " 'Establish Justice' which will insure 'domestic tranquility, promote the general welfare and secure the blessing of liberty' to women and to posterity" (p. 144). It is this appeal to the principles of the Declaration of Independence and the Constitution that characterizes the ideology of nineteenth-century American feminism and sets it on the path of seeking legal and political redress. Yet again, Sarah Grimké goes a step further and points to the sexual oppression of woman as the root cause of her subordination. "Legislation can do much towards producing that harmonious cooperation of the sexes which by the establishment of equal rights to person and to property will release woman from the horrors of forced maternity and teach her partner to subject his passions to the control of reason" (p. 145). This extraordinary sentence sees male sexual dominance as the primary evil and legislated equality as a means to end it. "The horrors of forced maternity," on which Sarah Grimké expands in her notes and elsewhere in her writings, is the nineteenth-century euphemism for marital rape, and the exhortation to men to subject their passion to the control of reason expresses the analysis of sexuality shared by many nineteenth-century woman's rights advocates.

Sexuality for purposes other than procreation needed to be severely controlled to keep marriage pure and harmonious. It was male sexuality that threatened the safety of the home through adultery, marital rape (which resulted in too frequent pregnancies for women), and the dangers of venereal disease. Men should be converted to the female view of restrained sexuality through appeals to reason, to "higher motives," and to Christian duty.[6] Sarah Grimké added to these idealistic appeals the practical argument that women who had economic and legal independence within marriage would be able to make their views prevail. These ideas are further elaborated in her notes on "Marriage."

An analysis of woman's situation that put emphasis on her sexual subordination to men had characterized the writings of Frances Wright and of the Owenite wing of British reformers in the 1840s. Historians had assumed that American feminist thought had been quite untouched by Wright's brief career on American soil and that the connection to British Owenite thought did not really appear until the last quarter of the nineteenth century. American feminist theory, as it developed in its early stages, was strongly influenced by the tradition of the American Revolution and emphasized legal and constitutional remedies for the wrongs of women's situation. Thus, even as late as the turn of the century, suffragists and Free Lovers stood in opposition to each other. Ellen DuBois has called our attention to a "Free Love" document written by Elizabeth Cady Stanton that dates from 1870,[7] and Stanton's unorthodoxy and advanced analysis of woman's sexual oppression have been justly praised by modern historians, even though they were denounced by Stanton's contemporaries. The Grimké documents point us to an earlier, and perhaps continuous, tradition of such an analysis among some American feminists. The way in which Sarah Grimké blends both views, arguing the need for legal and political as well as for sexual reform, is uniquely her own and merits the attention and further study of historians. The discovery of the Anglo-American connection in this Grimké document lends it greater significance and should inspire more searching comparative studies regarding the origins of feminist thought.

§➳§➳§➳

SISTERS OF CHARITY[8]

That the relative position that men have occupied has been a necessary position I hold to be as self-evident that kings and conquerors once held rightful sway over the people, but as soon as the illusion is dispelled which clothes them with imaginary superiority the basis on which their power and their authority rests crumbles away and a new organization of society is demanded to meet the exigencies of the age.

The leading error which has pervaded society has been the idea that but one class of persons can exist, live, think and act for themselves, that in them is concentrated the thinking power of the age, whereas in truth they are but a part of the rays which converge to a focus from the universal thought.[9]

It cannot be denied that the present state of society needs reformation. Various expedients have been tried, but as a sensible writer remarks we have not yet tried the experiment of giving to Women the same political Rights as men and throwing open to them all the civil and ecclesiastical offices—"In our hospitals, prisons, almshouses, lunatic asylums, workhouses, reformatory schools, elementary schools, Houses of Refuge—every where we want efficient women."[10] No one who has visited such institutions, where by the way we are admitted as a favor, none of these institutions requiring in their by-laws that women should be associated with men as overseers etc. etc., but must perceive the absolute need of women as coadjutors. Even those who feel the importance of this union of the masculine and feminine element regard it as a dernier resort to be tried as an experiment, rather than the carrying out of a law which has its foundation in the very nature of man, ignoring this vital fact to the best welfare of society that without union of labor between the sexes nothing can be well done, because there is nothing done which does not affect the interests of both. The apostle uttered a great truth applicable to all the work that has to be done for Humanity—"Neither is the woman without the man, neither the man without the women."[11]

"Women in the midst of all the splendor of a luxurious Home have perished by a slow wasting disease of the body and mind because they have nothing to do—no sphere of activity commensurate with the large mental powers or passionate energy of character with which God had endowed them. Send such a woman to her piano, her novels, or her cross stitch; she answers with despair."[12]

It must be conceded that there is an absolute necessity for the industrial sphere of women to be enlarged. Sewing machines are depriving thousands, if not millions of their daily bread. Bless the inventor of sewing machines, although present misery may be the result, as is the case in all changes however beneficial, yet this invention will do a grand work in elevating woman, it will impose upon her the necessity of seeking other occupations and whatever widens the sphere of usefulness adds to the intelligence of the class thus pushed onward and outward.

It is most unjust for any individual to make his feelings, or his opinions a standard for others, it betrays a most lamentable narrow mindedness and an utter want of interest in the welfare of the race—the question before one is vital to our progress and is worthy [of] the most thorough examination not on the grounds of sentiment and prejudice, but on the grounds of true philosophy, *common justice*, humanity—Such persons close their eyes and ears to the fact that unless honest employment is found for women they must be driven by starvation and despair to dishonest and unworthy if not infamous means to preserve life.

"Every injustice is a form of falsehood, every falsehood accepted and legalized, works in the social system like poison in the physical frame, and will taint the whole body politic through and through, ere we have learned in what quivering nerve, or delicate tissue to trace and detect its fatal presence. Human Laws which contravene the laws of God are not laws but lies, and like all lies must perish. There is a saying that a lie believed for half an hour might cause a century of mischief. What then is likely to be the effect of these laws which have existed as part of our common law for centuries—laws which may well be called lies inasmuch as they suppose a state of things which has no real existence in the divine regulation of the world? Laws which during all that period have tended to degrade woman in the eyes of man, interfered with the sacredness of the domestic relations, and infected the whole social system." "I regard these laws as one cause of prostitution, because in so far as they have lowered the social position of woman, they have lowered the value of her labor, and have thus exposed her to want and temptation which would not otherwise have existed.["]¹³

["]Far beyond the palpable visible working of these laws, cruel as they are in individual cases, lies an infinitely greater mischief in their injurious effect on the manners of the people," "they permeate, and vitiate the relations of the two sexes throughout the whole community."[14]

"Is it not rather absurd to devise as an antidote to the working of these laws, another law really as unjust in its way, which punishes a man for ill treating the creature he has been authorized to regard as his inferior? Every act of legislation, which takes for granted antagonism between the mas[culine] and fem[inine] nature, has tended to create that antagonism."

["]When the creator endowed the two halves of the race with ever aspiring hopes, ever widening sympathies, ever progressive capacities—when He made them equal in the responsibilities which bind the conscience and in the temptations wh[ich] mislead the will, He linked them inseparably in an ever extending sphere of duties, an ever expanding communion of affections—thus in one simple, holy and beautiful ordinance binding up at once the continuation of the species and its moral, social and physical progress.["]

"It is indisputable that the mutual influence of the two sexes—brain upon brain—life upon life—becomes more subtle and spiritual and complex, more active and intense in proportion as the human race is improved and developed. Physiologists know this well."

"I have the deepest conviction founded not merely on my own observation and experience, but on the testimony of some of the wisest and best men that to enlarge the working sphere of woman, to give her a more practical and authorized share in all social arrangements, which have as their object the amelioration of evil and suffering, is to elevate her in the social scale, and whatever renders womanhood respected and respectable in the estimation of the people tends to humanize and refine them."[15]

[The following reference to the Crimea refers to Florence Nightingale (1820–1910), who took a group of nurses with her to care for the British soldiers wounded in the Crimean War (1853–56).] In the Crimea "All bear witness to the salutary influence exercised by the lady-nurses over the men. In the most violent attacks of fever and delirium when the orderlies could not hold them down in their beds, the presence of one of these ladies, instead of being exciting, had the effect of calming the spirit and subduing the most refractory. It is allowed that these ladies had the power to repress swearing and bad and coarse language; to prevent the smuggling of brandy into the wards; to open the hearts of the sullen and desperate to contrition and responsive kindness."

"Whether in the strain of overwork, or the steady fulfillment of our arduous duty there was one bright ray . . . —the respect, affection, and gratitude of the men. No words can tell it rightly, for it was unbounded and so long as we stayed among them it never changed. Familiar as we were become to them, in and out day and night, they never forgot the respect due to our sex and position. Standing by them in bitter agony when the force of old habits is great, or by those in the glow of returning health, or walking up the wards among orderlies and sergeants, never did a word which could offend a woman's ears fall upon ours. Even in the barrack yard passing the guard-room or entrance, where stood groups of soldiers smoking and idling the moment we approached all coarseness was hushed; and this lasted not a week or a month, but the whole of my twelve months residence and my experience is that of my companions."[16]

Miss Nightingale had long studied all that fitted her for the great work she undertook and the soldiers at once recognized a master mind and bowed before it. Her studies had been what our mothers and grandmothers might have called unfeminine even masculine perhaps. Why this last was made a term of reproach we are at a loss to discover but how great was the power she exercised in consequence.

Had not this great occasion been presented to her, that power of intellect and christian benevolence . . . would never have had its full scope and we should still be twaddling about the "true sphere of women." "Women's work is wherever there is a good work to be wrought, and for this she should be educated: a mind so fortified would be in no danger of falling into the follies which the stringent etiquettes of society have been invented to curb" "and should be emancipated from the eternal tutelage in which the law insists on holding her."[17] What is the natural inference to be drawn from these facts with regard to the influence of woman in political and civil life? I wish it to be understood that I only advocate intelligent women as eligible to office just as I would [intelligent] men. . . .

Do you doubt the capability of Eliz[abeth] Fry to frame laws for the better regulation of Prisons, and the Reform of the Criminal Code, or of Caroline Chis[h]olm to alter and amend those relating to Emigration or of Mary Carpenter who has become an authority in all that concerns the treatment of juvenile delinquents?[18] Each of these women was "assailed by the bitterest animosity, and the most vulgar abuse, by those who condemned them and would have put them down merely as women." They have outlived prejudice and jealousy.[19]

It is to the pale scholar over his midnight lamp not the successful general, that we look for the improvement of the human race, and when the leaders of the age are those whose physical frame is assimilated more especially to the feminine phase of life, why sh[oul]d idle prejudice any longer shut out women from taking their place wherever intellect rather than strength is required. It will not be till the business of the world is more equally distributed that either sex will thoro'ly fulfill its vocation in life, or that we can hope for that harmonious cooperation which can alone make any great undertaking successful. At present women are depressed by the laws, depressed by a public opinion resulting from the laws, depressed by a public opinion resulting from the laws, depressed by the prejudice of parents and guardians, till the greater part of the sex is ignorant of its powers." . . . "Our present lack of accomplished statesmen and legislators may be traced to the unrepealed barbarism of ancestral laws which have retained the mothers of the nation in a degraded position. . . ."[20]

The laws respecting married women are one of the greatest outrages that has been perpetrated against God and humanity. To couple the highest and holiest institution, an institution connected not merely with the perpetuation of the race but with the most sacred instincts, the holiest affections, the noblest aspiration of our being, an institution designed above all others to bring the sexes into harmony, to educate not only the married pair but their offspring for a more exalted life—to couple such an institution on the one side with injustice and oppression and on the other with the loss of self-respect, independence and degradation is an insult to omnipotence and to the divinity he has conferred upon man, which has no parallel. Unless marriage becomes a grand and holy institution, unless birth be invested with the consecration of the Divine Presence, it is in vain to expect domestic felicity. There may be kindness on one side and subservience on the other, but the snakey coil will still entwine itself around the hymeneal altar and the hiss of the reptiles be heard mingling with the voice of love. I have used strong language, I feel deeply, strongly because I have seen the terrible effect of these laws on noble minded women, even where the husbands did all in their power to annul them. It was impossible not to feel that their rights were ignored and that they enjoyed the privileges they had, not by right, but by courtesy.

The laws respecting women are a blasphemy against God, they invade his right to decide on the equality of Human Rights and charge him with surrendering the duties and obligations, the conscience and the will of half his intelligent creation to the caprice, selfishness and physical superiority of the other. "Can you wonder that poisonous reptiles nestle and harbor their scaly loathsomeness in the very bosom of the marriage contract and hiss and rattle and rear their hooded heads, and whet their venomed fangs securely there."[21] These things must be, my brethren, until you teach woman self-respect and self-reliance by giving her just and equal laws, by raising her from her present degraded and abnormal position. The law which gives women the right before marriage to make the most important far reaching contract which a human being can make and then by legal enactment proclaims her incapable of the most common business contracts is too absurd to need any comment. Is there anything to hope for the world under the existing laws? Why hold we to these dead symbols of barbarism? We need laws now inspired by the vitality of the present era—laws bounding with the life blood of advancing civilization. If we would go on from glory to glory as a nation, [l]et us not borrow or reenact the laws of a barbarous age, but give utterance to the present revelation of Jehovah and invest woman with the halo which omnipotence designs for her brow. What an unwise man said of books viz. that it would be better for the world if every book were destroyed, may be said of the laws respecting woman. If every one of these enactments were obliterated the world would be better for it." . . .

"Fossils" are elegantly termed "the medals of creation"—Laws may with equal truth be called the medals of legislation, they are chronometers which tell the evolution thro' which society has passed. They mark distinctly the march of civilization and betoken with unerring certainty the condition of mankind in that distant period when hardly anything else remains to tell us what we have been. Laws characterize certain epochs. In some of them we see the rude and savage state of infant society, in others the attempts of some educated minds to rise above the barbarism of the times. I have no fault to find with past legislation. I believe it was in every age adapted to the then circumstances of the race. When physical force was man's highest honor, when like the wild man of the woods his reputation kept pace with the number of murders he committed, his laws were [as] bloody as his sword. By slow and painful experiences he learned to be less hostile to his brother man and we see in the codes of all civilized nations a gradual amelioration of the Laws, and those which were once in force, like the footprints of birds in red sand-stone, only exist to tell that they have been. . . .

Man can never legislate justly for woman because "he has never entered the world to which she belongs."

Woman seeks to give to our laws an inward security and strength (and permanence) which is infinitely more important than any outward restraint; in fact the former is the only firm and durable basis of the latter. It is self evident that inequality of Rights creates antagonism and the assumption that we must continue in this state is productive of nothing but evil, because the privileged and the oppressed stand in opposition to each other, the latter yielding unwillingly the distinctions which the former demand and the former shutting themselves up in the self made circle of their superiority and scorning even to examine the claims of the dependant class. How shall these two classes harmonize? The answer is simple. "Establish Justice" which will insure "domestic tranquility, promote the general welfare and secure the blessings of liberty" to women and to posterity. "Then the differences which exist between them in matters of small moment would readily disappear before their equality in those higher privileges on wh[ich] they set supreme value."[22] This state of things must be actualized, for it is impossible to lull the awakened soul into a belief that it is free when the galling fetters still clank around it. It is impossible for any woman of lofty purpose and pure morality to accept the dogma that woman was made to be subservient to man.

Thus far woman has struggled through life with bandaged eyes, accepting the dogma of her weakness and inability to take care of herself not only physically but intellectually. [S]he has held out a trembling hand and received gratefully the proffered aid. She has foregone her right to study the laws and purposes of the government to which she is subject. But now there is awakened in her a consciousness that she is defrauded of her legitimate Rights and that she never can fulfill [sic] her mission until she is placed in that position to which she feels herself called by the divinity within. [H]itherto she has surrendered her person and her individuality to man, but she can no longer do this and not feel that she is outraging her nature and her God. There is now predominant in the minds of intelligent woman to an extent never known before a struggling after freedom, an intense desire after a higher life. Let us not imagine that because superstition, blind faith in unexamined and untenable dogmas are losing their power over the mind of woman, that her religious nature will be swept away. Far from it. The fact that woman has eaten the bitter fruits of slavery to the will and selfishness and passions of man has prepared her to receive the truth of her own selfhood, revealed to her by the spirit of God. Hitherto there has been at the root of her being darkness, inharmony, bondage and consequently the majesty of her being has been obscured, and the uprising of her nature is but the effort to give to her whole being the opportunity to expand into all its essential nobility.

Legislation can do much towards producing that harmonious cooperation of the sexes which by the establishment of equal rights to person and to property will release woman from the horrors of forced maternity and teach her partner to subject his passions to the control of reason. Oh how many mothers have I heard say, I did not want this child, I am unable to do my duty to so many children and this feeling is a gangrene to my happiness. Think ye parents, what a welcome awaits the helpless, hapless being, the offspring of lust, not of sanctified affection, who is thus ushered into existence. Do I plead for woman? No, I plead for the race, because I see th[at] an endless curse hangs over humanity so long as marriage is thus misunderstood and desecrated.

"Suffering" says Cousin, "is the most excellent of all things."[23] I am inclined to think the philosopher is right, but for the suffering thro' wh[ich] woman has passed as the mother of the race, she would not now feel so keenly the wrongs inflicted upon her nor estimate, as she now does, how treasonable it would be to herself and humanity longer to keep silence. Woman by surrendering herself to the tutelage of man may in many cases live at her ease, but she will live the life of a slave; by asserting and claiming her natural

Rights, she assumes the prerogative which every free intelligence ought to assume, that she is the arbiter of her own destiny. . . . [S]elf reliance only can create true and exalted women.

Chemistry had invested a breath of air, a drop of water with such glory that days, for aught I know weeks, or months have been spent in their examination. Is woman, the mother of the race, less worthy of being studied and understood? Great truths that have hitherto been hidden are assuming the importance they merit and the equality of the sexes in all natural Rights is one that claims the attention of every reasoning mind. Health depends upon the inhalation of pure atmospheric air and the health of society depends no less upon the inhalation of truth. If human beings are pent up in a vitiated atmosphere we all know the terrible results, as exhibited in that horrible den of iniquity, the slave ship. The body politic exhibits now the ghastly and disfigured features of those, who die a loathsome death by breathing putrefied air. The laws which ages ago were good for the people are no longer so and the convulsions in society which are every where apparent are only the agonized throes of human beings who are dying for want of fresh air and sunshine. Change characterizes organic and inorganic bodies and the highest creations of God, his intelligent beings, are as much and as necessarily the subjects of change as any other part of his Creation. Every age has its own spirit. It is only by incessant change that the granite rock is formed, or that the majestic boabub [sic] rears its trunk and spreads out its branches, for change is the parent of stability. [E]very moment millions of the constituent cells of our bodies are dying and new ones coming in their stead, death is but the cessation of this change.

Religion which reason sanctions will stand the test of change and we shall be exhibiting "elevated philosophy, and charities of social life—sympathy, benevolence, domestic affections, self-sacrificing attachment" of wife and mother, of sister and daughter to a degree even superior to that she has already manifested. She can no longer receive the superstitions whose death warrant her reason has signed but she is awakening to higher and clearer ideas of her own nature and capacities and responsibilities. The debasing and unsatisfying babble of representation through another, of the beauty of feminine delicacy and dependence, has had time to echo and reecho itself . . . she has listened to it, paid homage to it—she is weary of it, she feels its emptiness with reference to that inward life which is not yet utterly extinguished.[24]

The law of might makes right. A distrust in woman gave birth to the old domestic policy; it has had its iron reign. Let us not censure it— let us even believe it did the best it could, that it designed and did bless humanity, but let not the past tyrannize over the present when the spirit has departed from it. Liberty is the breath of God. . . .

NOTES

1. Diane Worzala, "The Langham Place Circle: The Beginnings of the Organized Women's Movement in England, 1854–1870" (Ph.D. diss., University of Wisconsin–Madison, 1982).
2. Mrs. Anna Jameson, *Sisters of Charity, Catholic and Protestant, Abroad and At Home* (London: Longman, Brown, Green and Longmans, 1855). This book was reprinted in the U.S. in 1857 (Boston: Ticknor and Fields).
3. *Ibid.* Grimké gives no page numbers for this citation.
4. Since the opening quotation marks are missing in the original, I believe this to be Sarah Grimké's comment. No such citation could be found in Jameson.
5. Sarah Grimké was inconsistent in placing quotation marks around cited material. In the original handwritten manuscript there is an opening quotation mark several lines above the lines cited here, but it lacks the end quotation mark just above the lines I have cited. We could not identify the subsequent paragraph in Jameson. Moreover, it is heavily revised, with words crossed out and rewritten, all of which speaks for it being an original text by Sarah Grimké. I am convinced that it is.
6. For an excellent discussion of this position, see Linda Gordon and Ellen DuBois, "Seeking Ecstasy on the Battlefield: Danger and Pleasure in Nineteenth Century Feminist Sexual Thought," *Feminist Studies* 9, no. 1 (Spring 1983): 7–25.
7. Ellen DuBois, "On Labor and Free Love: Two Unpublished Speeches of Elizabeth Cady Stanton," *Signs* 1, no. 1 (Autumn 1975): 257–68, esp. 265–68.
8. WELD MSS. Handwritten notebook.
9. First quote, Sarah Grimké, "Condition of Woman," exerpt from notebook no. 3; second quote, Sarah Grimké, excerpt from an unpublished essay. Both quotes are taken from the WELD MSS.
10. Quoted in Jameson, *Sisters . . .* , 62, no source identified by Jameson or Grimké.

11. Compare: Neither was the man created for the woman; but the woman for the man. 1 Cor. 11:9.

12. Jameson, *Sisters* . . . , 99–100.

13. The following footnote is by Sarah Grimké: This is the opinion of a man of large experience, Mr. F. Hill, for many years inspector of prisons. He observes that the sin and misery alluded to would probably be greatly diminished if public opinion no longer upheld the exclusive spirit by which most of the lucrative employments are restricted to the male sex, whereby the difficulties with which females have to contend in earning an honest livelihood are greatly increased—"Crime its Amount, Causes and Remedies, by F[rederick] Hill Inspector of Prisons" (London: John Murray, 1853).

14. West[ern] Rev[iew], Jan. 57. Note by Sarah Grimké. This paragraph was moved forward in the manuscript, as per Grimké's direction.

15. The sources for the preceding quotations could not be identified.

16. The above paragraph was moved forward from its original place in the manuscript. Sarah Grimké cited it "Eastern Hospital. V2. p. 178." The full citation is [Frances M. Taylor] *Eastern Hospitals and English Nurses: The Narrative of Twelve Months Experience in the Hospitals of Koulali and Scutari by A Lady Volunteer*, 2 vols. (London: Hurst & Blackett, 1856), I: 180–81.

17. This section has been moved from a later place in the manuscript.

18. Elizabeth Fry (1780–1845), prison reformer; Caroline Chisholm (1808–77), concerned with the welfare of British emigrants to Australia, and Mary Carpenter (1907–77), educator and founder of a reformatory for girls.

19. Footnote by Grimké: En. Wo. Journal-Employments of Wo. P. 8. Edu. Wo. Ad. Sat. July 10, 3d page.

20. See n. 4.

21. The source of this quotation is not known.

22. The source of this quotation is not known.

23. Victor Cousin (1792–1867), French educator, philosopher, and historian.

24. The intended place of this paragraph in the manuscript is not clear.

❧ 16 ❧

SMG, Letter Draft
to George Sand

The two letters below illustrate Sarah Grimké's continuing involvement with feminist women in other countries. Her translation of Lamartine's *Joan of Arc* undoubtedly arose from her work as a teacher of French and her desire to make the heroine she so much admired more accessible to her pupils. As for George Sand, she had not only read her autobiography, but several of her books. In Sarah's book of clippings, usually handwritten, there are a number of excerpts from the writings of George Sand.

❧ ❧ ❧ ❧

Sarah M. Grimké, handwritten notes on a half sheet of paper. I identify it as draft of a letter she wrote to George Sand, because of the comments in the letter to Elizabeth Smith Miller that follows.

Permit a stranger to address you who knows you through your autobiography, which I perused with equal great interest and instruction and delight. There for the first time I found expressed my own views of the sacredness of marriage and maternity. Since then those views have been given to the American public in a work entitled "Woman and her Era" by Mrs. Farnham. I wished very much to send you this work when it first appeared, but could not find any way of doing so without putting you to the expense of paying for it thro' the mail after it had reached France by steamer. The author endeavors to prove that woman is superior to man—her reasoning has not convinced me of this, altho' I am a thoro' believer in the equality of the sexes, but those parts of her work which treat on marriage and maternity and prostitution were to me deeply interesting. Perhaps the work may have reached Paris and you may have seen it.

But Mrs. Farnham and her book are not at present the moving cause of my addressing you. I need help and I knew no one who would be so willing to aid me as yourself. I have lately been making a translation of Lamartine's Joan of Arc. I am an enthusiastic admirer of the Maid, I may almost say a worshipper—she seems to me no more of this world than was Jesus, if we except him, the most sublime specimen of humanity recorded in history, the grandest, purest medium of divine communication the world has ever seen. I am very anxious to obtain the best (so called) likeness of her. I do not suppose there is any authentic likeness. I have one, a profile, the head inclined, with a helmet on. I refer to the one in Lamartine [illeg] and there is more inspiration and sublime devotion in it. I have however read such stirring accounts of the statue modelled by the Princess Marie in the halls of Versailles that I suppose that is the true embodiment of this marvellous being. I cannot find in [illeg] N.Y. any photograph of that statue. If there is one it could be sent in a letter. I should esteem it a great favor if you would send it to me for my little volume.

I feel, dear Madame, that you will excuse my troubling you. Accept the sincere esteem and admiration of Sarah M. Grimké.

Sarah Grimké to Elisabeth Smith Miller, March 19, 1867.

. . . "I have been making a translation of Lamartine's "Joan of Arc.""* . . . I gave the manuscript to a friend who had it published, which I was unable to do myself. But my sole aim in getting it printed was to revive the memory of this extraordinary woman, to hold up to view an example of faith, courage, fortitude & love rarely equalled and never surpassed. . . . I had the boldness to write to

* Sarah M. Grimké (trans.), Alphonse M. L. de Prat de Lamartine, *Joan of Arc: A Biography* (Boston: Adams & Co., 1867).

Mme George Sans [*sic*] and tell her of my translation and request her to obtain said photograph [of a Joan of Arc statue] for me. I have not heard from her, so conclude, either that my letter miscarried, or that she does not think it worth while to notice the unknown presumptuous individual who addressed her. Nevertheless I am among her warm admirers [in] spite of her leaving her husband. . . .

❧ 17 ❧

SMG to Sarah Wattles

This letter, written during Sarah's stay at Raritan Bay Union, offers a rare glimpse into the way Sarah was influenced by her reading.

Thomas Buckle, in his essay "The Influence of Women on the Progress of Knowledge,"* gives a historical overview of progress in the status of women. He asks, "What is woman's influence on the 'progress of knowledge?' " (p. 169) and states, "It must be confessed that none of the greatest works which instruct and delight mankind, have been composed by women." Still, he believes "that they are capable of exercising, and have actually exercised, an enormous influence. . . . [This] works as an under-current below the surface . . . and has affected the shape, the character, and the amount of our knowledge." (p. 171)

He reasons: "Our knowledge is composed not of facts, but of the relations which facts and ideas bear to themselves and to each other; and real knowledge consists not of an acquaintance with facts, which only makes a pedant, but in the use of facts, which makes a philosopher." (pp. 172–73)

Women, argues Buckle, exert influence over how scientific discoveries are made. They are not enabled to make these discoveries themselves. From this he develops a sharply gendered theory of

* Henry Thomas Buckle, *Essays* (New York: D. Appleton Co., 1877).

152

knowledge. Women are "more emotional, more enthusiastic, and more imaginative than men. . . . They possess more intuition. They cannot see so far as men can, but what they do see they see quicker." [180] Women are kept from using their talent for induction by "that preposterous system, called their education, in which valuable things are carefully kept from them, until their fine and nimble minds are too often irretrievably injured."[181]

Citing mothers' influence on their talented sons, he argues, "I firmly believe that the imagination will effect quite as much as the understanding. Our poetry will have to reinforce logic, and we must feel as much as we must argue." [208]

Sarah was strongly influenced by his arguments for a gendered mind, for a male and female way of thinking, but proceeded to take these ideas in a feminist direction, arguing for women's superiority.

§➥§➥§➥

Orange, Dec. 27, [18]58

My beloved Sarah

. . . I have lately read with great pleasure the lecture on the "Influence of Woman on the Progress of Society" by Thomas H. Buckle. He shows I think conclusively that Woman has been the chief elevator of the race, that she must necessarily be so, because she has a finer organization and a clearer quicker perception of the beautiful and the good. Woman intuitively perceives a truth and reasons from the inward to the outward and establishes her position by facts. Man seeks for facts and from them deduces his theory. He shows that the deductive, or female mode of arriving at Truth is higher than the deductive or masculine mode. He brings some fine illustrations to prove this and shows that some of the greatest discoveries in science were made by deductive reasoning. This subject is continuing to claim the increased attention of some of the noblest minds and deepest thinkers of the age. Buckle remarks that Woman being thus highly gifted, it is of the greatest importance to the progress of the Race that the peculiar endowments she possesses should receive the highest cultivation, that she may fulfil [sic] the great end of her creation in humanizing and spiritualizing the world. The time has come when she is needed, and when her influence is of such paramount importance to the world, that all who desire the progress of the race should bend their energies to her full development. I am more and more persuaded that Woman is not only the equal of man, but his superior, that had it not been for the inner life of woman the race would have been utterly brutified. Man in becoming a father ministers to his lower nature. Woman in becoming a mother submits to the means by which the great mystery of birth is brought about, that she may enjoy the highest of all privileges that of moulding an immortal being, or more frequently she submits to it as a necessity, imposed by the right marriage is supposed to confer on the husband of absolute property in the person of the wife. The spiritual life which woman possesses in a superior degree to man saves her offspring from that utter degradation which would otherwise befall mankind. As soon as woman *feels* that no legal enactment, no superior physical strength ought to take from her the ownership of her person, that to become a mother is the holiest act she can perform, there will be human beings of another stamp, of a higher physical organization and mental structure. I speak you will doubtless understand of marriage as it is generally understood and entered upon in the world. . . .

ARTICLES

❦ 18 ❧

The Grimké Sisters and the Struggle Against
Race Prejudice

Articles 18 and 19 are included in this book because they bear directly on the significance of Sarah Grimké's work. While they deal mostly with the antislavery work of both sisters, this work was so crucial to the intellectual and political development of Sarah Grimké that it is inseparable from her later writings and thought.

"The Grimké Sisters and the Struggle against Race Prejudice" is an article I wrote before I entered graduate school. It is the first article in the field of history I published. What I then wrote is still valid, and I have nothing to add to it. The term "Negro" was then current (in 1963) and is therefore reprinted without alteration.

"The Political Activities of Antislavery Women" was written in 1976 and is here reprinted without editorial changes as a historiographic document. Since then there has been much scholarly interest in antislavery women and their activities, which is, of course, not reflected in the notes to this article. Additional evidence of widespread female petitioning in the antebellum period has tended to support the main thesis of this article: that women long before suffrage was gained were active agents in the political discourse of their time.

The discovery of the relationship of the Grimké sisters' 1837–38 tour to the building of female antislavery societies was made serendipitously. Long after the publication of my Grimké biography, I decided to research female antislavery petitions in the Library of

Congress. I was at that time contemplating writing a book on female antislavery societies. The petitions in the LOC are filed chronologically by the day they arrive in Congress; thus, petitions coming from particular localities are kept together, if they were submitted by one petition-gatherer. As I leafed through these petitions and made a note of their place of origin and date of origin, something sounded familiar to me, but I could not identify it. After several hours, it suddenly clicked—the places and times followed exactly the places and times of the Grimké sisters' tour. When I was back home, I consulted the calendar of their tour I had made and found that my hunch was right. By comparing the list of the places at which they had spoken with my list of female antislavery societies and the dates of their origin, I was able to trace with some precision the long-range effect of the sisters' tour. Out of sixty-seven towns and villages in which the sisters had lectured, thirty-four sent petitions to Congress within the next six months. And in eight towns new female antislavery societies were founded as a direct result of their trip. Their influence was undoubtedly greater than even these figures indicate, for they helped women reformers to network with one another and to form an organizational infrastructure which supported and materially subsidized the antislavery effort.

§❧ §❧ §❧

THE GRIMKÉ SISTERS AND THE STRUGGLE AGAINST RACE PREJUDICE

The outstanding role played by Sarah and Angelina Grimké in the struggle for abolition and woman's rights has only in recent years begun to be fully appreciated.[1] Carolina-born aristocrats and slaveholders turned abolitionists, they were and remained the *only* Southern white *women* in the abolition movement. As the first American-born women to make a public speaking tour, they opened the way for women to take part in public affairs.[2] As the first female anti-slavery agents, they early saw the connection be-

Reprinted from *The Journal of Negro History*, volume XLVIII, no. 4 (October 1963). By permission of the Association for the Study of African American Life and History (ASALH) Inc.

tween civil rights for Negroes and civil rights for women.[3] Sarah Grimké's pamphlet, *The Equality of the Sexes and the Condition of Women*, represents the first serious discussion of woman's rights by an American woman.[4] An integral part of all this activity was their life-long struggle against race prejudice, which deserves special attention.

Having intimate personal knowledge of the workings of slave society, they saw very clearly that slavery could be maintained in a Christian, democratic nation only because the myth of the Negro's inferiority served as an apologetic rationale. Angelina Grimké recorded a personal experience illustrating this, which involved her younger brother Henry:

> I have been suffering for the last two days on account of Henry's boy having run away, because he was threatened with a whipping . . . and yet . . . I am constantly told that the situation of slaves is very good, much better than that of their owners. . . . No wonder poor John ran away at the threat of a flogging, when he has told me more than once that when Henry last whipped him he was in pain for a week afterwards. I don't know how the boy must have felt, but I know that the night was one of agony for me; for it was dreadful not only to hear the blows, but the oaths and curses Henry uttered went like daggers to my heart. And this was done, too, in the house of one who is regarded as a light in the church. . . . I was directed to go to Henry and tenderly remonstrate with him. . . .
>
> He very openly acknowledged that he meant to give John such a whipping as would cure him of ever doing the same thing again and that he deserved to be whipped until he could not stand.
>
> I said that would be treating him worse than he would treat his horse.
>
> He now became excited, and replied that he considered his horse no comparison better than John, and would *not* treat *it* so. . . . I felt so much overcome as to be compelled to seat myself or rather to fall into a chair before him, but I don't think he observed this. . . . [5]

In this case she managed to convince her brother to let his slave return home unpunished. But Angelina Grimké never forgot the horror of discovering that her brother regarded a slave as less than his horse. She and Sarah carried on a relentless struggle against race prejudice on a programmatic, organizational and personal level all their lives.

Their programmatic attack on race prejudice found expression in their writings and speeches.

Angelina Grimké's *Appeal to the Christian Women of the South* stands alone in its indictment of slavery from a Southern woman's point of view and in its direct appeal to women to defy the slave laws. She bases her argument on behalf of the slave on the Bible and the Declaration of Independence. The core of her argument is her belief in the manhood and equality of the slave and in his *natural* right to freedom.

> . . . man, who was created in the image of his Maker, never can properly be termed a *thing*, though the laws of the Slave States do call him 'a chattel personal'; *Man*, I assert, *never* was put *under the feet of man*, by that first charter of human rights which was given by God. . . . [6]

Sarah Grimké, in a later article, elaborates on this theme:

> Cruelty is inseparable from Slavery; the one cannot exist in a community without the other . . . because there is a continual effort on the part of the master to reduce to a *thing* an immortal and intelligent human being, and an unwearied exertion on the part of the slave to maintain his manhood. [7]

Angelina closes her *Appeal* with a call to rebellion against the slave system, urging the white women of the South to pray, speak and act against slavery. Specifically: if they own slaves, they should set them free. If they cannot do so, they should pay them wages and educate them. If the law forbids it, "such wicked laws ought to be no barrier in the way of your duty."[8] Such laws should be broken.

In stressing the human rights of the slave, the Grimké sisters raised the level of discussion above the prejudiced position which regarded the slave as "the white man's burden."

> . . . as a southerner [sic], I *know* that I never could express my views freely on the abominations of slavery, without exciting anger, even in professors of religious. It is true *"the danger, evils and mischiefs* of slavery" could be and were discussed at the South and the North. Yes, we might talk as much as we pleased about *these* as long as we viewed slavery as a *misfortune* to the *slaveholder* and talked of "the dangers, mischiefs and evils of slavery" to *him*, and pitied *him* for having such a "sad inheritance entailed upon him." But could any

man or women ever "express their views freely" on the SIN of slavery
at the South! I say, never! Could they express their views freely as to
the dangers, mischiefs and evils of slavery to the *poor suffering slave*!
No, never![9]

If the Negro was entitled to equality on the grounds of his humanity, it followed that equality was his *right*, not a privilege to be
granted him at the slaveholder's pleasure. Angelina discusses this
question in detail in her polemical exchange of letters with Catherine
Beecher, the daughter of Lyman Beecher, who, from the stance of a
gradualist "friend of the slave," attacked her for her radicalism and
extremist views.

> . . . Now if every man has an inalienable right to personal liberty
> it follows that he cannot rightfully be reduced to slavery. . . . To make
> a slave is man-stealing . . . to hold him such is man-stealing—the
> *habit*, the permanent *state*. . . .
> Human beings have *rights* because they are *moral beings*; . . . as all
> men have the same moral nature, they have essentially the same
> rights. These rights may be wrested from the slave, but they cannot be
> alienated: his title to himself is as perfect *now* as is that of Lyman Bee-
> cher: it is stamped on his moral being, and is, like it, imperishable.[10]

From this analysis the Grimké sisters developed their attack on
race prejudice. It led them to expose the Colonization Society as an
instrument for depriving free Negroes of their rights and retarding
the freeing of the slaves. In this they followed the argument developed by Theodore Weld during the Lane Seminary debates and
gave respectful attention to the opinion of the leaders of the free
Negroes of Philadelphia, men such as James Forten and Robert
Purvis.[11]

Angelina wrote:

> . . . That the Colonization Society is a *benevolent* institution we deny.
> . . . And it is a perfect mystery to me how men and women can *con-
> sciously* persevere in upholding an association, which the very objects
> of its professed benevolence have repeatedly, solemnly, constantly and
> universally condemned. . . . Yes, the free colored people are to be ex-
> iled, because public opinion is crushing them into the dust; instead of
> their friends protesting against that corrupt and unreasonable preju-
> dice, and living it down by a practical acknowledgment of their right
> to *every* privilege, social, civil and religious which is enjoyed by the

white man. I have never yet been able to learn how our hatred to our colored brother is to be destroyed by driving him away from us. . . .

Surely you never want to "get rid" of people whom you *love*. . . . It is because I love the colored Americans, that I want them to stay in this country; and in order to make it a happy home to them, I am trying to talk down, and write down, and live down this horrible prejudice. Sending a few to Africa cannot destroy it. No—we must dig up the weed by the roots out of each of our hearts. . . . [12]

In their *Letter to Clarkson* published in 1837 the sisters forcefully stressed that "Northern prejudice against color is grinding the colored man to the dust in our free states, and this is strengthening the hands of the oppressor continually."[13]

Their belief in the inherent equality of the Negro as a moral human being led the Grimké sisters directly to adopting the demand for immediate emancipation. Angelina strongly suggested that gradualism stemmed essentially from race prejudice. In her *Letters to Catherine Beecher* she spells out what she means by emancipation: freedom for the slave, the payment of wages for his labor, legal rights, education and the protection of equitable laws. Then she asks:

Now why should not *all* this be done immediately! . . . I have seen too much of slavery to be a gradualist. I dare not. . . . Is there any middle path in this reformation! Or may we not fairly conclude that he or she that is not for the slave, in deed and in truth, is *against* him, no matter how specious their professions of pity for his condition![14]

The educational and propagandistic contribution to the antislavery movement made by the Grimké sisters and Theodore Weld in their collaboration on *American Slavery As It Is*, a powerful exposé of slavery based on eyewitness accounts and items culled from the Southern press, has been dealt with elsewhere.[15] It was the major propaganda weapon of the abolition movement until the publication of *Uncle Tom's Cabin*, which is partially based on information gathered in this book.[16] Here, one aspect of Angelina Grimké's contribution to this work is pertinent, namely, her eye-witness testimony.

In the course of my testimony I have entered somewhat into the *minutiae* of slavery, because that is a part of the subject often overlooked, and cannot be appreciated by any but those who have been

witnesses, and entered into sympathy with the slaves as human beings. . . . *One who is a slaveholder at heart never recognises a human
being in a slave.*[17]

Stressing not only the brutalities and horrors, but the "utter disregard of the comfort of the slaves in little things," Angelina records
that slaves, to her knowledge, were deprived of bed and bedding,
allowed no mosquito nets in a tropical climate, fed only twice a day
and never at a table, not allowed to leave the house without permission, separated from their families, humiliated needlessly and
constantly watched. Her acute awareness of these "little things" is
rare even among abolitionists; her testimony concerning the daily
realities of slave life is unique, coming from a white Southern
woman.

Not satisfied to express themselves only through their speeches
and pamphlets, Angelina and Sarah Grimké carried their attack on
race prejudice into their organizational activities.

As a young woman of eighteen, Angelina left the Episcopal
Church and joined the Presbyterian Church of Charleston, S.C.,
where she became very active, taught large Sunday school classes
and initiated inter-faith work among women. Her minister, Rev.
William McDowell, was a Northerner who had only recently come
to Charleston; Angelina therefore expected that he would support
her in her anti-slavery views. When she challenged him, he readily
admitted that he considered slavery a great evil but that to abolish
it would create even worse evils. The only thing one could do was
to pray and wait. Angelina suggested one could "pray and work,"
and followed this up by asking him to preach in church next Sunday
just as he had spoken to her now. This, Rev. McDowell did not feel
he could do. Somewhat disillusioned with a man whom she had up
to then greatly admired, Angelina proceeded to speak to the church
elders, all slaveholders, at one of their meetings.

> They listened with courtesy, told her that young as she was it was
> not strange that she should feel thus, but that riper years and wider
> experience would surely set her right.
>
> She then turned to private members. One mistress of slaves said,
> "Slavery has embittered my whole life." Another, "It is the greatest
> curse to us, but I see no possible escape." Another said, "I sympathize
> with you, but cannot see a ray of hope."

After long working and waiting, hopeless at last of action by her church, she felt that it could be her church no longer, and that to continue in it was to partake of its guilt.[18]

Angelina stopped attending the Presbyterian Church and was thereupon brought before the Synod for "neglect of the publick worship of God in his house" and similar charges. She was treated with consideration and respect by the Elders, but was officially expelled on the basis of the charges. The subject of slavery was not mentioned in the proceedings.[19]

Angelina then began to worship with the Quakers in Charleston. Sarah urged her to come North to live, but Angelina decided to stay because she wanted to act against slavery "where it was . . . to act directly upon it by example, testimony and personal effort."[20] She spent the winter of 1828 trying to induce her friends and relatives to alleviate the lot of their slaves, and constantly aired her antislavery views. This led to so much friction and ill feeling that she finally concluded it was impossible to act effectively against slave society while living within it. Self-imposed exile was her final gesture of protest in the South.

In Philadelphia, both sisters became members of the Society of Friends. Sarah, for many years, prepared herself for the Quaker ministry. Apparently they cultivated an acquaintance with the few colored families attending their Quaker meeting, for, by 1837, the Douglass family and especially Sarah Douglass were among their close friends.[21]

It is quite obvious from their letters that they were disturbed by discriminatory practices within the Society of Friends for some time before expressing their views. They did not protest the practice of segregated seating until after they had joined the Quakers, which they did largely because of the latter's strong antislavery position. But they were newcomers, inexperienced in the ways of the Society. Moreover, there were strong personal ties linking them with several of the most influential Quaker Elders in Philadelphia, who had befriended them since their arrival in the city and offered them hospitality. All of which did not prevent them from becoming aware of the gap between anti-slavery ideals and actual practice in the Orthodox Philadelphia Society of Friends. Gradually, their disillusionment increased. Early in 1837 they expressed their sympathy with Sarah Douglass "in thy sufferings on account of the cruel and unchristian prejudice which thou hast suffered so much from. . . . "[22] At about the same time they seated themselves on the "Negro bench" in protest against segregated seating. Later that year, Angelina wrote to Sarah Forten, daughter of James Forten, and asked her to cite her experiences with race prejudice and to give her ideas on Colonization. Sarah Forten replied in a lengthy and frank letter and Angelina, in her speeches and articles, made good use of the information she supplied.[23] In a letter to a friend Angelina complained that Philadelphia Quakers did "absolutely nothing" for the colored people:

> We attended their last Monthly Meeting of Managers and believed it right to throw before them our views on prejudice. No colored sister has ever been on the board and they have hardly had any colored men. . . . [24]

When Angelina wrote her *Letter to Garrison* and later her *Appeal*, the Quaker hierarchy expressed disapproval of such public and "unwomanly" action. A little later, when Sarah once again was rebuffed in a Quaker meeting in her efforts to speak, she gave up all ideas of the ministry and felt that her "bonds were broken." She was so embittered by the long conflict that she wrote a statement about it, the publication of which, she felt, would undoubtedly lead to her disownment. Theodore Weld considered it too controversial for the American Antislavery Society and it was never printed.[25]

Both sisters were finally disowned by the Quakers because of a technicality—Angelina's marriage out of the faith and Sarah's attendance at the wedding. Similar to Angelina's expulsion from the Presbyterian Church, this was merely the formal ending of a long period of disillusionment and struggle with the orthodoxy. There can be little question that their antislavery views and activities were the major source of contention.

Early in 1839 their British Quaker friend, Elizabeth Pease, asked the Grimké sisters to furnish any facts they might have concerning discrimination within the Society of Friends in America, so that British Friends might bring pressure to bear to end such practices. Sarah Grimké wrote to Sarah Douglass and asked her

... to make any statements which will answer her purpose, such as thy mothers treatment at friend Snowdens funeral, the case of thy cousins at North meeting and the facts whatever they may be relative to the "bench for colored persons." ... State the circumstances that occurred in N.Y. both to thy mother and thyself.[26]

Sarah wrote a 40 page letter to Elizabeth Pease on April 10, 1839, in which she included the reply received from Sarah Douglass and cited all the facts known to her.[27] Parts of this letter, omitting all names, were printed in England in a pamphlet, *Society of Friends: Their Views of the Anti-Slavery Question, and Treatment of the People of Colour*. Later, when the Quaker William Bassett was preparing his defense in proceedings which ended in his disownment by the Quakers because of his abolitionist activities, Sarah induced her friend to furnish him with the same facts she had previously supplied.[28]

While lecturing in New York, Angelina wrote a friend concerning the Ladies' Antislavery Society of New York:

... on account of their strong aristocratical feelings ... they were most exceedingly inefficient ... We had serious thought of forming an Anti-Slavery Society among our colored sisters and getting them to invite their white friends to join them, in this way we think we could get the most efficient white females to join them.[29]

She also urged her "colored sisters" to attend the forthcoming convention of antislavery women and speak up on the subject of prejudice.

Both sisters were active in leadership at the First Anti-Slavery Convention of American women, which met in May 1837 in Philadelphia. They frequently presented their views, offered resolutions and were elected to office. They played this role at all conventions they attended, usually offering very specific recommendations on combatting prejudice, such as the one presented by Sarah Grimké at the 1838 convention:

Resolved ... that it is ... the duty of abolitionists to identify themselves with these oppressed Americans by sitting with them in places of worship, by appearing with them in our streets, by giving them our countenance in steam-boats and stages, by visiting them at their homes and encouraging them to visit us, receiving them as we do our white fellow citizens.[30]

By and large, the antislavery women showed a greater awareness of the implications of prejudice than their contemporaries: their meetings were integrated; they braved mobs frequently and developed the tactic of "non-violent resistance" by walking out of a mob, arm-in-arm, one Negro woman and one white; they gave their Negro members a chance to take leadership positions. Yet, the mere fact that such resolutions had to be presented and debated year after year shows that even their understanding left something to be desired.

Angelina had prepared an *Appeal to the Women of the Nominally Free States* for the 1837 convention, which she read to the assembled gathering. A committee was appointed to revise the statement, which was published as a pamphlet by the convention and widely circulated, both North and South. In it, Angelina particularly stressed the bond of women of all races:

> They [the female slaves] are our country-women—*they are our sisters*; and to us as women, they have a right to look for sympathy with their sorrows, and effort and prayer for their rescue. . . .

Again, she was very specific:

> Treat them as *equals*, visit them as *equals*, invite them to cooperate with you in Anti-Slavery and Temperance and Moral Reform Societies—in Maternal Associations and Prayer Meetings and Reading Companies. . . . Multitudes of instances will continually occur in which you will have the opportunity of *identifying yourself with this injured class* of our fellow beings; embrace these opportunities at all times and in all places. . . .

Then she appealed to her "colored sisters":

> We are aware of the prejudice you suffer daily, but entreat you to bear with us in our folly. You must be willing to mingle with us whilst we have the prejudice, because it is only by associating with you that we shall be able to overcome it. You must not avoid our society whilst we are in this *transition* state. . . . We entreat *your aid* to help us overcome it.[31]

This level of understanding of the complexities of race relations was unfortunately rare in her day, even among staunch abolitionists.

Sarah and Angelina Grimké carried their principles into their private lives. They had been, legally, slaveholders although they had personally always refrained from owning slaves. During one short period of her youth, before her anti-slavery sentiments had become a matter of firm conviction, Angelina had accepted the ownership of a slave named Kitty, whom she hoped to re-train and rehabilitate. In this she succeeded, but found the situation so painful that she soon transferred ownership back to her mother. After moving North, the sisters anxiously tried to persuade their mother to free her slaves. Mrs. Grimké refused, but promised to leave them the four slaves remaining to her as their inheritance; after her death, they might do with them as they wished. This arrangement was carried out and the four slaves were eventually freed.[32]

One of these slaves, Stephen, presented a complex problem. Stephen's wife and children were owned by a different owner in Charleston. Mrs. Grimké had for some time permitted Stephen to hire out his services and to live with his wife, or at least visit her frequently. Stephen suddenly developed fits of violent madness; his wife's owner refused him permission to enter the premises and Mrs. Grimké placed him in the almshouse, there being no other facility available for the care of sick slaves. When she wrote to her daughters about this, Angelina and another sister living in Philadelphia, Mrs. Anna Frost, decided to buy Stephen from their mother and bring him North, so that he might recover under adequate care. In this case Mrs. Grimké was willing to part with the slave's services. The sisters made an effort to purchase Stephen's family as well, but were refused by the owners. Stephen, once out of the almshouse and apparently sufficiently recovered to do light work, refused to leave his family. Thus the situation remained, with Angelina regularly paying her mother for his maintenance at a period of her life when she and her family were in serious financial difficulties. Finally, for reasons not revealed in the correspondence, Stephen decided to come North. Angelina took him into her home, where he was supposed to make himself useful. Due to his continuing ill health, bad work habits and a surly disposition, he proved to be a problem. The sisters blamed not him, but his life in slavery for these difficulties and considered it their duty to rehabilitate him, no matter how difficult and unpleasant the process might be. Although it took a long time, they finally succeeded. Stephen, by then an old man, was settled on a little truck farm near Philadelphia, which he rented and operated so success-fully that he was much respected by his neighbors. They referred to him as a "hard-working, industrious man." In 1846, when An-gelina visited him, she reported:

> Stephen gave us a most hearty welcome, treated us to oranges, cakes, sugar plums and mineral water.

During her visit she helped him negotiate the purchase of his little piece of land and advanced him the purchase money.[33]

In similar fashion the sisters tried to keep in touch with and aid all the former family slaves, frequently sending money South for them. They made great efforts to transcend the attitude of benevo-lence and charity which such relationships of necessity implied and to establish a relationship of equals on purely human terms. Whether they succeeded or whether it actually was possible to suc-ceed in such an approach within a country still partially a slave society must remain a matter of conjecture.

A relationship of quite a different order was the life-long friendship of Sarah Grimké and Sarah Douglass. The two had met at Quaker meetings and shared the experience of working in the Philadelphia Fe-male Anti-Slavery Society. There is hardly anyone, other than her sis-ter Angelina, to whom Sarah Grimké wrote more frankly and fully concerning her most intimate thoughts, strivings and hopes. Simi-larly, Sarah Douglass consulted her friend before her engagement and marriage, later shared with her her womanly troubles in what turned out to be an unhappy union. She visited the Weld-Grimké home in Belleville, staying for several weeks. The Grimké sisters never came to Philadelphia without visiting the Douglass household.[34]

The marriage of Angelina Grimké and Theodore Weld was a care-fully planned, inter-racial affair. It was held in the home of Mrs. Anna Frost, the elder sister of Sarah and Angelina, in Philadelphia. Mrs. Frost, while anti-slavery, was not an abolitionist and strongly objected to some of the sisters' activities and writings. Another sister, Elizabeth, who had remained in Charleston, wrote to Angelina when she heard of her marriage plans:

> . . . in your letter to Mother you speak of all colors being present, I would only ask the question if something is not due to sister Anna's feelings and opinions on this subject. . . . [35]

Similar sentiments were expressed by the mother. Nevertheless, wedding plans proceeded. The cake was ordered from a colored confectioner who used "free sugar." The guests included in addition to Garrison and most of the leading abolitionists, Sarah and Grace Douglass and Betsy Dawson and, probably, her daughter, two former Grimké slaves.[36] Sarah Grimké described the affair in a letter:

> . . . We all felt that the presence of a magistrate, a stranger, would be unpleasant to us at such a time, and we therefore concluded to invite such of our friends as we desired and have the marriage solemnicized . . . in a religious and social meeting. . . . A colored Presbyterian minister then prayed, and was followed by a white one. . . . The certificate was then read by Wm. L. Garrison and was signed by the company. . . . Several colored persons were present, among them two liberated slaves, who formerly belonged to our father, had come by inheritance to sister Anna, and had been freed by her. They were our invited guests, and we thus had an opportunity to bear our testimony against the horrible prejudice which prevails against colored persons. . . . [37]

That this wedding was considered a scandal, even among their personal friends, is shown by a letter Angelina wrote to an old friend a few months later:

> . . . I am sorry thou still has so much trouble in vindicating our characters for daring to have such a wedding. . . . [38]

The abolitionist newspaper *The Emancipator*, in reporting on the riots which ended in the burning of Pennsylvania Hall by a mob, stated that one excuse for the riot was that "amalgamation" had been practiced in Philadelphia.

> . . . one rumor held that Mr. Weld at his recent marriage had six whites and six blacks for groomsmen and bridesmaids. Another that 500 blacks and whites were seen promenading on Chestnut street. . . . [39]

It was during this riot that Angelina Grimké Weld, a bride of a few days, made her last public speech, in a hall surrounded by a howling mob.

The most spectacular testimony of the Grimké sisters against race prejudice came late in their lives. Sarah was seventy-six and Angelina sixty-three when they discovered the existence of two colored nephews, sons of their brother Henry and one of his slaves. They were horrified to learn that the two young men and their mother and brother had been left by Henry in his will as slaves to his white son, Montague, and had only been freed by Federal troops. Two of them, Archibald and Francis, had come North and were studying at Lincoln University, where they were making brilliant records. The sisters and Theodore Weld decided at once to accept these newly-found nephews as members of the family, offering them every advantage such a relationship implied. Angelina wrote to them:

> ...I am glad you have taken the name of Grimké. It was once one of the noblest names of Carolina. You, my young friends, now bear this *once* honored name. I charge you most solemnly ... by your upright conduct and life-long devotion to the eternal principle of justice and humanity and religion, to lift this name out of the dust where it now lies, and set it once more among the princes of our land.[40]

Accompanied by her son, Angelina attended her nephews' commencement exercises at Lincoln. She and Sarah helped the nephews to complete their college education. Since they were not financially able to do so on their own, they solicited contributions from other abolitionists for their "Archie-fund." This was one of the last subjects on which Sarah expressed her concern shortly before her death.

What had started as a "sacred duty" soon became a warm family relationship. The nephews considered the Weld home their own, accepted the help and guidance of their aunts and later paid tribute to the lasting influence these two women had had on their lives. They amply justified the confidence put in them. Francis James Grimké graduated from Princeton Theological Seminary in 1878 and, for almost fifty years, pastored the 15th Street Presbyterian Church in Washington, D.C. He was a trustee of Howard University and a member of the American Negro Academy. His collected works, four massive volumes of sermons, essays and letters, testify to his militant and articulate leadership. Archibald Henry Grimké, after graduating from Harvard Law School in 1874, practiced law in Boston, wrote and lectured extensively for Negro rights and published biographies of Garrison and Sumner. He served as an alternate delegate to the Republican National Convention (1884), Consul to Santo Domingo (1894–1898), President of the American Negro Academy, and won numerous distinctions and honors, including the 1919 Spingarn medal of the

NAACP. By his own definition "a liberal in religion, a radical in politics and the race question," he was one of the outstanding Negro leaders of his day.

There is symbolic beauty in the relationship of these two white women and their Negro nephews, which culminated their life-long struggle against race prejudice. If the better world of brotherhood and equality, in which they so firmly believed, could not be realized within their lifetime, the Grimké sisters bore witness that individuals in their private lives could realize such brotherhood. In this, as in their writings and speeches, Sarah and Angelina Grimké have left us a heritage well worth cherishing.

NOTES

1. G. H. Barnes and D. L. Dumond (eds.), *Letters of Theodore Dwight Weld, Angelina Grimké Weld and Sarah Grimké, 1822–1844* (Appleton-Century, 1934), 2 vols. Hereafter referred to as LET. Also: D. L. Dumond, *Antislavery* (Ann Arbor: University of Michigan Press, 1961); E. Flexner, *Century of Struggle* (Cambridge: Harvard University Press, 1959).

2. Frances Wright, the first woman to lecture in this country, was a Scotswoman. The first U.S.-born woman speaker was a free Negro woman, Frances Maria W. Stewart, who delivered four addresses in Boston in 1832–33. See Flexner, 343, n. 10, and L. O'Connor, *Pioneer Women Orators* (New York: Columbia University Press, 1954).

3. They were trained and appointed as part of the "seventy," agents of the American Anti-Slavery Society, although they were never paid agents. See Dumond, 193 and fn.

4. Flexner, 344, n. 19.

5. Angelina Grimké, *Diary*, WELD MSS, Weld-Grimké Papers, William L. Clements Library, University of Michigan, Ann Arbor. Any letters from this collection will hereafter be referred to as WELD MSS. See also Catherine Birney, *The Grimké Sisters* (Boston, 1885).

6. Angelina Emily Grimké, *Appeal to the Christian Women of the Southern States* (New York, 1836).

7. *Anti-Slavery Record*, vol. III, no. 1 (Jan. 1837), 2.

8. A. Grimké, *Appeal* . . .

9. A. E. Grimké, *Letters to Catherine Beecher, in Reply to an Essay on Slavery and Abolitionism, Addressed to A. E. Grimké* (Boston: Isaac Knapp, 1838), 98.

10. *Ibid,*. 4, 115.

11. D. Dumond, *Antislavery*, 160–62, also chap. 14. Also: H. Aptheker (ed.), *A Documentary History of the Negro People in the United States* (New York: Citadel Press, 1951), 71–72, 145–46; R. Billington (ed.), *Journal of Charlotte Forten* (New York: The Dryden Press, 1953), Introduction.
12. A. Grimké, *Letters to C. Beecher*, 35–36, 40–41.
13. LET, vol. I, 368.
14. A. Grimké, *Letters to C. Beecher*, 12–13.
15. D. Dumond, *Antislavery*, chap. 30, and Benjamin Thomas, *Theodore Weld* (New Brunswick, N.J.: Rutgers University Press, 1950), chap. 12.
16. *Ibid.*, 332–33.
17. [Theodore Weld], *American Slavery As It Is: Testimony of a Thousand Witnesses* (New York: American Anti-Slavery Society, 1839), 57.
18. Th. D. Weld, *In Memory Angelina Grimké Weld* (Boston, 1880).
19. WELD MSS, Diary Angelina Grimké, 26–29; also WELD MSS, Letter William McDowell to Angelina E. Grimké, May 14, 1829.
20. Weld, *In Memory* . . .
21. Sarah Douglass was a greatly respected teacher; her mother, Mrs. Grace Bustill Douglass, conducted a millinery business. Her brother, Robert, was a portrait painter. See A. B. Smith, "The Bustill Family," *Journal of Negro History*, vol. X, no. 4, 638–44.
22. LET, vol. I, 363.
23. *Ibid.*, 379–81.
24. WELD MSS, Letter A. E. Grimké to Jane Smith, March 22, 1837.
25. LET, vol. I, 373, 414.
26. *Ibid.*, 744.
27. WELD MSS, statement by Sarah and Angelina Grimké, incomplete, April 10, 1839. Also: H. J. Cadbury, "Negro Membership in the Society of Friends," *Journal of Negro History*, vol. XXI, no. 2, 151–232.
28. LET, vol. II, 829–32.
29. WELD MSS, A. E. Grimké to Jane Smith, April 17, 1837.
30. Proceedings Anti-Slavery Convention of American Women, held in Philadelphia May 15, 16, 17 and 18, 1838. It is significant that this was one of the few resolutions not adopted unanimously.
31. A. E. Grimké, *Appeal to the Women of the Nominally Free States*, issued by an Anti-Slavery Convention of American Women (New York: W. S. Dorr, 1837), 62–63.
32. LET, vol. I, 471. Also: T. Weld, *In Memory* . . . ; C. Birney.
33. WELD MSS, A. Grimké Weld to Th. Weld from Philadelphia, May 27, 1846. The above passage regarding Stephen is based on correspondence in the WELD MSS covering the years 1838–46. The references are too numerous to be listed here.

34. The above is based on the correspondence in the printed letters and in the WELD MSS. See also Sarah Grimké Personal MSS, Library of Congress, 2 letters to Sarah Douglass, 1843.
35. Eliz. Grimké to A. E. Grimké, May 2, 1838, WELD MSS.
36. WELD MSS, Marriage certificate Theodore Weld-Angelina E. Grimké.
37. LET, vol. II, 678–79.
38. WELD MSS, A. E. Grimké to Jane Smith, July 7, 1838.
39. *Emancipator*, May 17, 1838, 11.
40. C. Birney, 292 and passim. Also: numerous letters in the WELD MSS, covering the years 1868 to 1872; Angelina Grimké Weld, "Biographical Sketch of Archibald Grimké," *Opportunity: Journal of Negro Life*, vol. III (Feb. 1925), 44–47; Anna Cooper, *Life and Writings of the Grimké Family*, n.p.

❧ 19 ❧

The Political Activities of
Antislavery Women

Historians of abolitionism have paid a great deal of attention to the
ideas, the personalities, the psychological and political motivation
of the abolitionists, and to the outcome of four decades or more of
agitation. There has been relatively little interest in an institutional
analysis of the antislavery movement except for the brief periods of
dramatic dissension within the movement.[1] Yet the phenomenon of
a movement which began with the dedicated band of sixty-two people who formed the American Anti-Slavery Society in 1833 and went
on to organize more than 1350 local societies in 1838; which in
1840 and 1844 entered politics with decisive, if negative, results and
which had by 1860 so affected public opinion that a Republican
could be elected President, deserves functional analysis.[2] Regardless
of whether abolitionism achieved its stated goals, there is no question that it served to transform public opinion on the issue of slavery

This essay was printed in Gerda Lerner, *The Majority Finds Its Past:
Placing Women In History* (New York: Oxford University Press, 1979),
and is here reprinted by permission. It is based on a paper delivered at the
southern Historical Association Meeting, Atlanta, November 11, 1976. The
essay has benefitted from the criticism of Professors Betty Fladeland, Eric
Foner, James McPherson, Anne Firor Scott, Ronald Walters, and Peter
Wood.

in the North and the West and that it did so by a series of organized efforts with different tactical goals.

Antislavery workers and agitators labored in groups; their societies were local organizations and county and state networks; the anniversaries and conventions served organizational, educational, and public relations functions. To change public opinion, antislavery organizations had to be visible locally, have continuity and a recognizable public face, and had to carry on some form of propaganda and organizing work. Such work formed the basis for fund-raising, recruitment of forces, political campaigning, even the bringing of law suits. The important groundwork out of which political antislavery would grow was laid in the years 1836–43. Antislavery petition campaigns were an important aspect of this work. Women, who played a crucial role in antislavery petitioning, had far more importance in transforming public opinion and thereby influencing political life than has hitherto been recognized.

Quite in keeping with the general neglect of the history of women, the antislavery activities of women have been slighted by historians. In so far as women abolitionists were singled out for closer scrutiny, interest focused on a few individual "leaders," their biographies and especially their psychology, with emphasis on their supposed deviance. Where organized female activity has been interpreted at all, historians have taken for granted the supposedly negative effect of the "woman question" in splitting the American Anti-Slavery Society in 1840.[3] Even historians of women have been more interested in the effect of antislavery activities on the rise of feminism than in the activities themselves.[4]

Men and women in the antislavery movement did not necessarily engage in the same activities nor approach their work in the same way. Thus the questions historians traditionally ask of their sources frequently fail to elicit material pertaining to the activities of women. Much antislavery historiography has been focused on leadership. Who were the antislavery leaders? Why and how did they come to the movement? How effective were they? Yet, three separate studies of antislavery leaders have defined leadership in such a way that it would be difficult for women to be included.[5] Among criteria for leadership were: representation at antislavery conventions (only male conventions were considered), political candidacy, frequent mention in the press, and membership in community organizations.

Given the social restraints on women, only the latter is applicable to women, and so it is no wonder that no woman appears among antislavery leaders in these books.

Yet in each community where there were antislavery societies there were women known as leaders. It is generally recognized that, except for a few wealthy contributors, women provided most of the financial support of the antislavery movement. Women sold and distributed literature: less noted is the fact that they also wrote such literature and served as editors for many of the antislavery papers.[6]

Dwight L. Dumond and Gilbert Barnes were the first historians to call attention to the pivotal effect of the 1837–39 petition campaign and to the role of women in it. But they regarded women's activities as merely auxiliary to those of men and failed to take into consideration the dynamic effect of the campaign in bringing large groups of women into political activity for the first time. This view of the subject has prevailed.[7]

A more recent study of women's antislavery petitions focuses on petitions from one small New York township and uses the signatures in combination with census data to construct a "profile" of the female antislavery activists—an interesting and useful analysis but one which tells us nothing about the impact of this activity on women and on the community.[8]

Disfranchised groups in a democracy can hope to influence those holding political power only by persuasion, by educational activity, and by exerting pressure in a variety of forms. Their peculiar relationship to political power, as the group longest disfranchised, caused women to use various methods of pressure and persuasion. Slaves, women, and some members of reform societies had petitioned since colonial days. Petitions and memorials against slavery had been used in the 18th century, but mass petitioning first occurred in the 1820s as part of the work of missionary societies. By 1830 petitions reached the House of Representatives in large numbers on such varied issues as the tariff, currency reform, the 10-hour day, abolition of Sunday mail, abolition of slavery, and opposition to the removal of the Cherokee Indians. The American Anti-Slavery Society took up petitioning in 1835–36 as an important means of educating Congress and the public.

Antislavery petitions began to flood Congress and were met in 1836 in the House by enactment of the "gag rule," which provided for tabling without further action all petitions on the subject of slavery. The "gag rules" passed by succeeding Congresses at the insistence of Southern Congressmen broadened the abolition campaign into a defense of free speech. The political effect was to widen the base of the antislavery movement.

The striving of women to organize separate societies and take part in antislavery activities was greatly spurred by British influence and example. British women had worked for passage of the 1833 Emancipation Act by petitioning activities starting in the early 1820s. The reformers Elizabeth Heyrick and the Quaker Elizabeth Fry, both active in public work for emancipation, were known and respected models for American women. The 1835 visit by the popular antislavery lecturer George Thompson, which had been financed by Scottish and British women's organizations, also had considerable impact. But in the frontier and rural regions these influences were not as significant in encouraging women to organize as was the actual petitioning experience of antislavery men and women.

As early as 1836, in her *Appeal to the Christian Women of the Southern States*, Angelina Grimké had pointed out that petitions were a particularly apt means of political expression for women, who were excluded from other means of influencing politics. She urged Southern women to take up petitioning and cautioned them not to be disappointed if progress was slow. "If you could obtain but six signatures to such a petition in only one state, I would say, send up that petition, and be not in the least discouraged."[9]

In May 1837 when the first Anti-Slavery Convention of American women met in New York City, female antislavery societies were clustered in only a few regions. In Massachusetts there were female antislavery societies as early as March 1833 in Reading, Boston, Groton, Amesbury, and Lowell. In 1834 female societies were formed in Salem, Newburyport, and Haverhill. In 1835 such groups organized in South Weymouth, Weymouth, Braintree, Dorchester, Lynn, Fall River, and New Bedford. The second cluster of organizations was in Pennsylvania, centering on Philadelphia. New York City had two active female societies of white women and one of colored women. After the convention societies were organized in scattered towns in Maine, New Hampshire, Rhode Island, Pennsylvania, Michigan, Connecticut, and upstate New York.[10]

The convention made petitioning the focus of their activities, but women first had to overcome traditional indoctrination and fear of disapproval. The convention addressed itself to the subject in a variety of ways. A resolution offered by Angelina Grimké stated that the right of petition was "natural and inalienable, derived immediately from God . . . whether it be exercised by man or woman. . . ." It urged "every woman . . . annually to petition Congress with the faith of an Esther . . ."[11] Apparently the appeal to divine and biblical sanction for petitioning did not convince all women present of the propriety of this activity. The convention engaged in spirited debate and a resolutions battle over the rationale for women's participation in what was clearly understood to be political activity. The radical position urging women to regard slavery as a "national sin because Congress has the power to abolish it" lost out to a more moderate resolution appealing to mothers to pray for the abolition of slavery for the welfare of their children.[12] Nevertheless, the convention proceeded in a businesslike way to organize its petition activity by taking pledges from delegates to send petitions for the abolition of slavery and the slave trade in the District of Columbia to each town in their several states in the course of the present season. Undertaking also to petition the various churches to take an antislavery stand and commending Rep. John Quincy Adams for his defense of the "right of petition for women and for slaves," the convention adjourned.[13]

In order to carry out the convention resolutions women had to organize in their communities, to set up a network of petition gatherers, letter writers, agents, and lecturers. The Anti-Slavery Conventions of American Women held in 1838 and in 1839 further intensified this campaign. Women sent hundreds of petitions to the Congress and thereby precipitated a political crisis in the fight against the gag rule and for the right of petition. In October 1837 the *Congressional Globe* reports Senator Wm. C. Preston of South Carolina as saying that 28,000 memorialists had subscribed to abolition petitions. Robert Walker, the Senator from Mississippi, found a majority were signed by females and children. He believed, "if the ladies and Sunday school children would let us alone, there would be but a few abolition petitions."[14] Mr. Walker underestimated the zeal of male petitioners, but he correctly perceived the importance of petitioning for the mobilization of abolition sentiment among women. By the end of 1838 these petitions were so numerous as to create a storage problem. A number of them were kept and are now in the National Archives, but most of those sent after 1840 were apparently destroyed.[15]

What follows is based on a hand count and analysis of 402 antislavery petitions sent to the 25th Congress in its three sessions in 1837–38.[16] These petitions in the National Archives are filed in the order in which they were received, which makes it possible to get a sense of the organizational sequence of the campaign. They are arranged by region and by the object of their appeal. During this period the major objects of the petitioners were: abolition of slavery in the District of Columbia; opposition to the annexation of Texas; and outlawing the internal slave trade. Most of the petition-signers signed all three petitions.[17]

Most of the petitions have a notation on the outside specifying the number of signatures, whether male or female; the name of the petition-gatherer (sometimes, and not so frequently, if female), and the place of origin.[18]

From areas where abolition societies made up of males predominated, the petitions came in, usually one from each town or county, with mostly the signatures of men. From Vermont came 24 petitions with 1792 male signatures and 671 female signatures; from Michigan three with 535 male and 120 female signatures; from Illinois five signed by 266 males and 66 females. (See Table 1.) It is evident from these petitions that women got involved in the campaign first through the encouragement of men, who asked their wives and daughters to sign petitions and help circulate them. Here and there female names appeared next to the names of male family members, indicating that they had been solicited by the male petition gatherer within the family circle. Another way was to have the female names on a separate sheet or on a petition divided in half vertically, with all the male names on one side, the female names on the other. This may indicate that males gave the petition to women to circulate among their friends or possibly their sewing circle or church group. The names of men and women never appear randomly mixed.

The old centers of antislavery activity, where strong female societies had flourished since 1833, provided most of the petitions. Pennsylvania and Massachusetts sent 280 petitions out of a total of 402.

It is not only absolute numbers but the pattern of distribution of female and male signatures which can inform us about the role

Table 1. Antislavery petitions sent to the 25th Congress (1–3 sessions, 1837–38, identifiable by sex of signer)

			Number of petitions			Signatures		
			Male signers only	Female signers only	Male/Fem. signers	Male	Female	Total
Origin	To	Total						
New York	House	15	8	3	3	2088	852	2940
Vermont	House	26	15	3	8	1792	671	2463
Ohio	House	50	30	4	16	4074	942	5016
	Senate	18	8	2	8	1463	247	1710
Illinois	Senate	5	3	2	—	266	66	332
Michigan	Senate	3	2	1	—	535	120	655
Totals		117	66	15	36	10,218	2898	13,116

played by women in the petition campaigns. For purposes of comparison, the petitions have been grouped into those with more male signatures (Table 1) and those with more female signatures (Table 2). Table 3 provides a summary of all the petitions, regardless of gender distribution.

When comparing Table 1 and Table 2, what is most remarkable is the ratio of male to female petition signers. In Table 1 the ratio is 3.3 male to 1 female signer; in Table 2 the ratio is almost exactly reversed—3.5 female to 1 male. In Table 1 female signers appear mostly on "mixed" petitions. In Table 2 female signers appear in great numbers on petitions circulated by women, while "mixed" petitions are relatively unimportant in accounting for the total. This reflects the organized activity of separate female antislavery organizations and can be seen most clearly in the 54 petitions sent to the Senate from Massachusetts: 53 petitions circulated by women account for 20,951 signatures, and one circulated by a man accounts for 29. A similar pattern can be seen in the four Pennsylvania petitions to the Senate, with 41 male signatures and 1754 female ones. As Table 3 shows, in the total number of signatures on 402 petitions, women signers outnumber men by better than two to one.

If we look at the origin of the petitions, it becomes obvious that female petitioning activity was correlated to the spread of female societies. Vermont, Illinois, and Michigan had few female societies: in New York City, where most of the New York petitions origi-

Table 2. Antislavery petitions sent to the 25th Congress (1–3 sessions, 1837–39, identifiable by sex of signer)

| Origin | Total number of petitions | *Number of petitions* | | | *Signatures* | | |
		Male signers only	Female signers only	Male/Fem. signers	Male	Female	Total
Massachusetts to House	173	78	83	12	8340	14,285	22,625
Massachusetts to Senate	54	1	53	—	29	20,951	20,980
Connecticut to Senate	5	—	—	5	625	908	1533
Pennsylvania to House	49	29	12	8	3020	4133	7153
Pennsylvania to Senate	4	1	2	1	41	1754	1795
Totals	285	109	150	26	12,055	42,031	54,086

nated, there were only three small and relatively inactive women's societies. Ohio is interesting, in that antislavery organization was strong, as can be seen by the large number of petitions; but it was unevenly distributed among Garrisonians in the Western Reserve and adherents of the American Anti-Slavery Society in other areas. The bulk of the petitions and those with the most signatures came from the Western Reserve and reflect the strength of Garrisonian abolitionism, which encouraged women to take an active and independent part in antislavery work.[19]

The petitions also reveal some interesting aspects of the way in which men and women carried on this work. It is not possible to say with absolute certainty who the petition circulators were in each case. Frequently the name of the petition gatherer is listed on the back of the petition and often the person is the first signator. Clearly, petitions with female signatures only were circulated by women. Given the prejudice against women's participation in public affairs, which permeated antislavery circles as it did society in general, one can assume that males would seldom solicit the signatures of females. If they did, they would do so within the family circle, as was indicated by one petition which was headed "5 women from Ash-

Table 3. Antislavery petitions sent to the 25th Congress (1–3 sessions, 1837–38, identifiable by sex of signer) Summary of petitions, by sex of signer

Total number of petitions		Total *number of petitions by sex*			Signatures		
		Male signers only	Female signers only	Male/Fem. signers	Male	Female	Total
Table 1	117	66	15	36	10,218	2898	13,116
Table 2	285	109	150	26	12,055	42,031	54,086
Total	402	175	165	62	22,273	44,929	67,202

Source: For all three tables: Petitions to the 25th Congress, 1–3 Sessions, House Records HR–25 A and Senate Records 25–H–H1, National Archives.

tabula County, Ohio—these signers are my wife, my son's wife and daughter of lawful age," indicating that this procedure was considered exceptional. Table 3 shows that men and women circulated sex-separated petitions in almost equal numbers (175 male; 165 female). Considering the overwhelming predominance of female signatures, it seems reasonable to assume that most of the 62 "mixed" petitions were also circulated by women.

There were a number of petitions which came from the same town, one circulated by a man, one by a woman. I made a separate count of the signatures in each case and found that the women's petitions always had more names than those of men. In comparing the way family names appeared on the petitions, a curious pattern emerged: the names of men of the same family would be randomly scattered among the signers on petitions circulated by a man, indicating that men circulated their petitions at the workplace or perhaps at meetings and only later—if at all—included male *family members.* The women's petitions would always show a cluster of family members, which indicates that women first gathered the signatures of all their female relatives and then moved on, probably house to house, to gather other women's signatures. One such petition was particularly moving—it showed the names of 24 women of the same family, headed by Lois Packard, who obviously was the matriarch—94 years old. Clearly, men and women, engaged in the same activity, went about it in different ways.

Analysis of antislavery petitions combined with a study of church affiliation, census data, and property records can reveal much about the women who engaged in the petitioning. Two recent studies have used this method to determine the religious affiliation and property standing of men and women who signed antislavery petitions. In articles analyzing two petitions from Sandwich, New Hampshire, Patricia Heard and Ellen Henle additionally find the same pattern I found in the petitions I analyzed: more women than men signers (260 women; 222 men). They also noticed that at least 23 wives signed, while their husbands did not, which may indicate the exercise of female autonomy or it may simply mean the absence of husbands. They also analyzed the route taken through the village by the petition gatherers and found that men and women followed approximately the same route.[20]

A more elaborate study by Judith Wellman of 304 upstate New York antislavery petitions sent in 1838–39 shows that 14.5 per cent of the petitions were signed by women alone (44) and 54.9 per cent were signed by men and women together. Wellman reasons that "women, either alone or with men, signed almost 70% (69.4%) of the petitions." This would support the findings in my sample.[21]

The predominance of women among petition signers shows that women sought to exert what political influence they could in the cause of antislavery. But what of the effect of petitioning on women? Is there evidence that it became an instrument of organizing and helped to draw women into greater involvement in antislavery? Was petitioning a one-time activity or did it lead women toward other reforms and broader political activities?

The sudden spurt of petitioning fervor growing out of the first Female Anti-Slavery Convention is obvious in the number and size of the petitions. When women begin to petition on their own we first see huge petitions such as "remonstrance of Lydia Maria Child and 3028 others, women of Boston, Mass." or "Sarah G. Buffum and 2832 women of Bristol County, Mass." or "H. Huntington and 1400 others, women of Lowell, Mass."

It was then also that petitions came in clusters, several from one town, or several towns in one county bundled together. This was the result of an organized drive with responsible coordinators in towns and counties, who gathered various petitions together before forwarding them to Washington. It reflected the level of organization, region by region, of female societies.

The Massachusetts petitions were particularly interesting. They began with a mammoth petition of 4054 women of Boston. On October 12, 1837, Daniel Webster presented petitions of the "citizens" (which must be taken to be male and female, since male petitions almost always state "male" or "voters").[22]

When one checks the list of Massachusetts towns from which petitions were received against the list of female antislavery societies in the state, it appears that almost every such society sent at least one petition; many sent more than one. There were petitions also from a number of towns that did not have societies; one can assume these were circulated by sympathetic individuals. When one checks the list of towns from which the petitions were signed against the list of towns in which the Grimké sisters had lectured during their 1837–38 lecture tour, the correlation is striking: out of 44 Massachusetts petitions, 34 came from towns in which the sisters had lectured. Conversely, out of 67 towns in which the sisters had spoken, 34 sent petitions to Congress within six months of their visit.[23]

The Grimké sisters' tour offers an interesting example of the way in which educational work, organizing, and petitioning were interconnected. The fourteen Massachusetts antislavery societies represented at the 1837 women's convention were probably the strongest of the state's female societies. Sarah and Angelina Grimké lectured in every town where there were female societies and in many others, speaking to at least 40,500 persons. As a direct result of their trip new female societies were formed in eight towns within six months of their tour: Concord, W. Bradford, W. Amesbury, Holliston, Andover, W. Newbury, Brookline, and Worcester, where they had been invited with the express purpose of helping to form a new society.[24] The old societies and the new were spurred in their petitioning activity by these lectures. The gathering of petitions, in turn, led to a growth in membership and local influence.* Women who signed

---

* The sisters kept accurate records of the first two weeks of their tour, recording the new members recruited at their meetings. At six meetings in the Boston area they reported 154 new members had been recruited. If anywhere near this level of recruitment was sustained during their other 82 meetings, Wendell Phillips was right in regarding their tour as an organizing success.

petitions once did not necessarily become active antislavery workers, but they would be likely to attend the annual antislavery fair or to contribute to it, thus spreading the financial base of the movement.

That petitioning immediately led to a widening of political influence can be seen in Massachusetts. In March 1838 Angelina Grimké brought a women's antislavery petition with 20,000 signatures before a committee of the Massachusetts legislature, and formally addressed the politicians. The importance of her presentation did not so much lie in the fact that she was the first woman ever to speak to an American legislature in behalf of women, as in the fact that she represented an organized network of female antislavery societies. Here was indeed a new force on the political scene, one which politicians had been forced to recognize as a pressure group. Massachusetts women continued to petition Congress, but the main force of their effort was directed to their state legislature. Early in 1839, petitions signed by more than 1400 women were presented to the Massachusetts House of Representatives, asking the repeal of all state laws which discriminated against Blacks and which outlawed interracial marriage. The petitions were met with scorn and ridicule, but provoked a lengthy debate in the House on the right and propriety of women petitioners. This debate only served to spur petitioning activity by women, and, although the ban on interracial marriages was not rescinded during that session, abolitionist pressure with active female participation continued, until the law was repealed in 1843.

Petition gathering was arduous work in which women had to brave opposition, ridicule, attack, and the disapproval of friends and neighbors. Juliana Tappan wrote about her experience:

> I have left many houses ashamed of my sex. . . . Ladies sitting on splendid sofas looked at us as if they had never heard of the word Texas and I presume some of them would have been unable to say . . . whether or not it belonged to the U.S.[25]

Another woman wrote of the apathy that met her efforts to form a female antislavery society in Connecticut:

> Women have been taught to depend on the men for their opinions. We had occasion to observe this in our efforts to obtain signatures to petitions; my daughter visited almost every house in this town for the purpose and found that it was the men generally, who needed

free discussion, for the women would not act contrary to the ideas of the male part of their family.[26]

A Massachusetts woman who had circulated the petition against the ban on interracial marriages reported opposition but was less disturbed by it:

> I suppose you heard of our *heretical* position. Many of its signers seemed troubled by the ridicule consequent upon it, but it strikes me as a nail which hit. . . . There is nothing like shocking people's prejudices sometimes. It reveals their extent and power and oft times works much good.[27]

Though the particular responses of individual women varied, petition gathering engendered self-confidence and assertiveness. It led many women toward increased participation in the public sphere. From petitioning their representative to canvassing the opinions of candidates prior to election was only a small step, one which women in New England and in Ohio took in the 1840 and 1842 elections. Some women campaigned for Whig candidates in 1840. Antoinette Brown and Lucy Stone took part in Gerrit Smith's campaign for Congress in 1852 and "had the pleasure of helping to bring about a successful issue of his campaign."[28]

Many abolitionist women supported antislavery candidates and took an active part in political campaigns. But the majority did not. After the 1840 split in the antislavery movement it is striking to note the decline in female participation in the Western & Foreign Anti-Slavery Society, which denied full participation to women. The New York City female societies virtually disappeared.[29] Judith Wellman in her study of antislavery petitioning activities in Oneida County, New York, has also noted a sharp drop-off in female participation in that region after 1840. While petitioning activity nearly doubled in 1850–51 (over 1838–39), the percentage of female signatures shrank dramatically: from 70 per cent of all signatures in 1838 to 2.3 per cent in 1850. In other words women had provided the bulk of the petition signers and circulators in 1838, but were a tiny minority of signers in 1850. Judith Wellman reasons that this is due to the fact that antislavery had shifted from a moral reform movement to a political one, a shift which by definition excluded women.[30] It is certainly true that the shift to political abolitionism discouraged female participation, as can be seen by looking at the regions in which the Garrisonian movement remained strong—Massachusetts, Pennsylvania, and Ohio. In those areas women continued to be publicly active and increasingly visible as petitioners, lecturers, and speakers. There is also good evidence, however, that many women, once they had become habituated to political activity through petitioning, transferred this activity to causes more directly connected with their self-interest. There were mass petitioning campaigns for women for equal property rights legislation in New York, Massachusetts, and Ohio in the 1840s and 1850s. With the convening of the first woman's rights convention at Seneca Falls in 1848 and with the subsequent biannual conventions in many states, women's political activity began to focus on woman's rights issues. The ancient method of trying to influence legislators and change public opinion by means of memorials was raised to new levels of significance. The resolutions, memorials, and appeals which issued from local, state, and national woman's rights conventions for more than seven decades became instruments of propaganda, education, and pressure. Equal in importance was their significance in helping to mould an ideology of feminism around which women's political activities could be rallied.

The final surge of women's antislavery political activity came in 1863 when the Women's Loyal National League was formed for the purpose of collecting one million signatures to a petition asking for passage of the 13th Amendment. That goal was not reached, but Senator Charles Summer presented a roll of petitions with 300,000 signatures, all of them collected by women.

One more aspect of women's petitioning activity needs to be considered: its function as a builder of antislavery strength in communities. Petitioning itself led to strengthened organization; fund-raising and distribution of literature followed from petitioning.

There is a good reason to believe that abolition sentiment and activity were carried out to a large extent by family groups. Abolitionist families were the base for support of the antislavery newspapers; they were the mainstay of the underground railroad; they provided continuity of ideas and beliefs, regardless of shifting tactics and organizational emphasis at various times. Members of antislavery families from New England furnished the core of abolitionist organizers and supporters in the Western Reserve of Ohio. Hicksite Quaker families spearheaded antislavery organization in Rhode Island and eastern Pennsylvania. Since women, in order to overcome the inhibitions and strictures against political activity, needed the support of their female relatives, it is not surprising to find family clusters among antislavery women. Judith Wellman found that of the female petition signers in 1836 in Paris township, Oneida County, New York, 42 percent had other family members who also signed petitions.[31] The membership list of the Ohio Ashtabula County Female Antislavery Society in 1835–37 also shows a high percentage of family groups. Out of 245 names checked, 89 (over 36 percent) were in family groups of 2–6 (counting only those with the same surname).[32] If one counted those actually related by family of birth, including married sisters with different surnames, the percentage would undoubtedly be higher. There can be little doubt that families in which the women were so strongly organized provided a strong supportive base for the antislavery politics of men. In Ohio and perhaps elsewhere these kinds of antislavery activities had considerable significance in building a reform tradition in certain families and localities which gave continuity to the reform impulse.

In summary, the petitioning activities of antislavery women in the 1830s and 40s were of far greater significance to the building of the antislavery movement than has been previously recognized. Moreover, these activities contributed directly to the development of a contingent of local and regional women leaders, many of whom were to transfer their political concerns to feminist activities after 1848. Further investigation of this aspect of reform should lead to a re-evaluation of antislavery history, which would give to women a less marginal place and see their work as an integral aspect of the antislavery movement.

NOTES

1. Dwight L. Dumond, *Antislavery: The Crusade for Freedom in America* (Ann Arbor, 1961), chap. 33.

For more studies of political antislavery see: Frederick J. Blue, *The Free Soilers: Third Party Politics, 1848–54* (Urbana, 1973); Eric Foner, *Free Soil, Free Labor, Free Men: The Ideology of the Republican Party before the Civil War* (New York 1970); Richard Sewell, *John P. Hale and the Politics of Abolition* (Cambridge, Mass., 1965); Theodore Smith, *The Liberty and the Free Soil Parties in the Northwest* (Cambridge, Mass., 1897); James B. Stewart, *Holy Warriors: The Abolition-*

ist and American Slavery (New York, 1976), and *Joshua Giddings and the Tactics of Radical Politics, 1795–1864* (Cleveland, 1969); Bertram Wyatt-Brown, *Lewis Tappan and the Evangelical War Against Slavery* (New York, 1969).

For emphasis on the impact of ideological and organizational division in the antislavery movement see: Gilbert H. Barnes, *The Anti-Slavery Impulse: 1830–1844* (New York, 1939), chaps. 15, 16; Aileen Kraditor, *Means and Ends in American Abolitionism: Garrison and His Critics on Strategy and Tactics, 1824–1850* (New York, 1967).

For a critical interpretation of abolitionists as anti-institutional see: Stanley Elkins, *Slavery: A Problem in American Intellectual and Institutional Life* (Chicago, 1959); Willie Lee Rose, *Rehearsal for Reconstruction: The Port Royal Experiment* (New York, 1964).

2. Figures based on Annual Reports of the American Anti-Slavery Society 1834–39, as cited in Louis Filler, *The Crusade Against Slavery: 1830–1860* (New York, 1960), 67.

3. Dumond, *Antislavery*, chaps. 33, 34 and Barnes, *Anti-Slavery Impulse*, chaps. 15, 16.

For a factual description of the schisms see: Filler, *Crusade Against Slavery*, chap. 6.

For a view minimizing the impact of the split of 1840 see: Gerda Lerner, *The Grimké Sisters from South Carolina: Rebels Against Slavery* (Boston, 1967); and Ronald Walters, *The Antislavery Appeal: American Abolitionism after 1830* (Baltimore, 1976).

4. See, for example, Eleanor Flexner, *Century of Struggle: Woman's Rights Movement in the United States* (Cambridge, Mass., 1959), and Keith Melder, *The Beginning of Sisterhood: The American Women's Rights Movement, 1800–1850* (New York, 1977).

5. David Donald, "Toward a Reconsideration of Abolitionists, in *Lincoln Reconsidered* (New York, 1956), pp. 28–36; Alice Hatcher Henderson, *The History of the New York State Anti-Slavery Society*, unpublished dissertation (University Microfilms, Ann Arbor, Michigan, 1963); Gerald Sorin, *The New York Abolitionists: A Case Study of Political Radicalism* (Westport, Conn., 1971).

6. The literature focusing on women in the antislavery movement is sparse. Except for a few biographies of female abolitionists, the subject is treated as a minor aspect of the general antislavery movement in separate chapters of the monographs cited in note 3 above. See also: Alma Lutz, *Crusade for Freedom: Women in the Antislavery Movement* (Boston, 1968); Jane H. and Wm. H. Pease, *Bound with Them in Chains: A Biographical History of the Antislavery Movement* (Westport, Conn., 1972), chap. 3 "The Boston Bluestocking: Maria Weston

Chapman"; William Loren Katz, "The Black/White Fight Against Slavery and for Women's Rights in America," *Freedomways*, Vol. XVI, No. 4 (1976), 230–36; Carol Thompson, "Women and the Anti-Slavery Movement," *Current History*, LXX (May 1976), 198–201. A recent book focusing on women abolitionists is: Blanche Glassman Hersh, *"The Slavery of Sex": Feminist Abolitionists in America* (Chicago, 1978).

7. Dumond, *Antislavery*, chap. 33; Barnes, *Antislavery Impulse*, chaps. 15, 16.

8. Judith Wellman, "To the Father and the Rulers of Our Country, Abolitionist Petitions and Female Abolitionists in Paris, New York, 1835–45," Unpublished paper, Berkshire Conference on Women's History, Bryn Mawr College, June 1976.

9. Angelina Emily Grimké, *Appeal to the Christian Women* (New York, 1836).

10. Dates based on the Annual report of the Board of Managers of the Massachusetts Anti-Slavery Society (Boston, Mass., 1838) and the Proceedings of the Anti-Slavery Convention of American Women, held in New York City, May 9–12, 1837 (New York, 1837).

11. Proceedings, 8.

12. *Ibid.*, 11–12.

13. *Ibid.*

14. *Congressional Globe*, 24th Congress, VIII, 337.

15. Barnes, *Antislavery Impulse*, 266, fnn. 34 and 39.

16. Petitions to the 25th Congress, 1–3 Sessions, House Records HR-25 A and Senate Records 25-H-H1, National Archives. Petitions to Congress 1821–38 were examined and scanned, but are not included in the count.

17. For a discussion of these petitions see Dumond, *Antislavery*, pp. 245–48. Dumond discusses 1496 petitions, but these are often duplicates as to the signatures, since he lists the totals for petitions on various antislavery topics. Thus, his figures and mine differ.

I chose to concentrate on the petitions opposing the annexation of Texas, considering this the most political issue of the time and the kind women would least likely be concerned with. I reason that whatever the number of women concerned with this issue, *more* women could be found signing petitions on other issues.

The 402 petitions I examined represent a random sampling of the larger total discussed by Dumond. I believe the sample is large enough to permit the making of generalizations as to patterns, but it would be desirable to do a more thorough study comprising all the petitions for a selected year.

18. A scan of the petitions revealed the pattern of origin and of male-female participation. The signature count on the outside of the petition was not always accurate; the errors were in omitting female names. Several petitions which listed "male" on the outside actually contained female names, probably an effort on the part of the petition gatherer to maximize the political pressure on his Congressman by making it appear that all signers were voters. This convinced me that if I accepted the outside notation and gender count, I would be erring on the conservative side, with respect to female participation.

   Petitions are designated "male" or "female" depending on the notation on the outside or the count inside. If persons of both sexes sign a petition it is here designated as "mixed."

19. For a detailed account of Ohio abolitionism see: Douglas A. Gamble, "Garrisonian Abolitionists in the West: Some Suggestions for Study," *Civil War History*, Vol. XXII, No. 1 (March 1977), 52–68; James Brewer Stewart, "Peaceful Hopes and Violent Experience: The Evolution of Reforming and Radical Abolitionism, 1831–1837," *ibid.*, Vol. XVII, No. 4 (Dec. 1971), 293–309.

20. Patricia Heard, "One Blood All Nations' Antislavery Petitions in Sandwich": *Fifty-ninth Annual Excursion of the Sandwich Historical Society*, Sunday, Aug. 27, 1978 (n.p., n.d.), 26–31; and Ellen Langenheim Henle, "Forget Not the Matron: Sandwich Women and Antislavery in the Antebellum Years," *ibid.*, 32–38. I am indebted to Dr. Ellen Henle for bringing this item to my attention.

21. Judith Wellman, "Are We Aliens Because We Are Women: Female Abolitionists and Abolitionist Petitions in Upstate New York." Paper presented to the National Archives Conference, April 1976. Unpublished.

22. Journal of the United States Senate of America, 1st Session, 25 Congress (Washington, D.C., 1837), 63, Oct. 12, 1837.

23. This is a conservative figure. There were five country petitions, which likely included some of the towns the sisters visited, but did not so designate.

24. For a more detailed account, see Lerner, *The Grimké Sisters*: chaps. 12–14.

25. Juliana A. Tappan to Anne Weston, July 21, 1837, Weston Papers, Boston Public Library.

26. Hanna H. Smith to Abby Kelley, July 25, 1839, Abby Kelley Foster Papers, American Antiquarian Society, Worcester, Mass.

27. M. E. Robbins to Abby Kelley, Jan. 21, 1839, *ibid*. The writer was the corresponding secretary to the Lynn Female Antislavery Society.

28. Antoinette Brown, Oct. 1852, Blackwell Family Papers, Box 54, Library of Congress.

29. Amy Swerdlow, "Abolition's Conservative Sisters: The Ladies' New York City Anti-Slavery Societies, 1834–1840." Paper presented at the Third Berkshire Conference on the History of Women, Bryn Mawr College, June 9–11, 1976. Unpublished.
30. Wellman, "Are We Aliens. . . . ," 7, 11.
31. Wellman, "Fathers and Rulers. . . ."
32. Minutes of the Ashtabula County Female Anti-Slavery Society, Manuscript, Western Reserve Historical Society, Cleveland, Ohio.